Motoring to War

Motoring to War

Accounts of Motor Vehicles from the Boer War
& the First World War

Motor Transports in War

Horace Wyatt

"Get There!" (Extract)

"Treat 'Em Rough!" (Extract)

E. Alexander Powell

The Dennis 30 cwt. Chassis

LEONAUR

Motoring to War
Accounts of Motor Vehicles from the Boer War & the First World War
Motor Transports in War
by Horace Wyatt
"Get There!" (Extract) and *"Treat 'Em Rough!" (Extract)*
by E. Alexander Powell
The Dennis 30 cwt. Chassis

FIRST EDITION

First published under the titles
Motor Transports in War
"Get There!"
"Treat 'Em Rough!"
The Dennis 30 cwt. Chassis

Leonaur is an imprint of Oakpast Ltd
Copyright in this form © 2013 Oakpast Ltd

ISBN: 978-1-78282-205-9 (hardcover)
ISBN: 978-1-78282-206-6 (softcover)

http://www.leonaur.com

Publisher's Notes

The views expressed in this book are not necessarily
those of the publisher.

Contents

Motor Transports in War

Contents

Introduction

By the editor of *The Autocar*

We have been told, and rightly, many times within the last few weeks that the present war is unique, not merely on account of the vastness of the contending armies, but also on account of the power of the weapons employed. In fact, the war has very properly been described as an engineer's war, and such, indeed, it is, as the engineer is wholly responsible for the tremendous development in every warlike instrument which has taken place since 1870. He is responsible, too, not merely for the development, but for the invention of wholly new methods of offence and defence. But his influence does not end here, and it is not merely in the firing line that one sees the influence of the engineer: even as this war is the first occasion on which modern weapons, explosives and projectiles have been tested on the grand scale, so, too, is it even more emphatically the first occasion on which motor transport has been thoroughly tested at all.

While the recent Balkan war, (as at time of first publication), provided a practical test of many of the weapons used in the great war today, motor transport played only a very small part in it; and it is very extraordinary that an innovation of this kind should be truly tested for the first time upon such a stupendous scale. It is the motor car, the motor van and the motor lorry which have rendered the rapid movements of the present war possible; it is not yet realised to the full how great have been the services of motor transport in the supply of ammunition and food to the troops, and in the rapid conveyance of the wounded to the hospitals. No one is better qualified than Mr. Horace Wyatt to deal with this new and important branch of modern warfare.

In his capacity formerly as editor and now as consulting editor of *Motor Traction* he has studied the question from its inception: from its small beginnings in British army manoeuvres many years ago right up to the present time he has followed the subject with the closest attention. Not only so: he has personally investigated the work performed by motor transport in the *grandes manoeuvres* on the Continent. I have had the good fortune to work closely with him for many years, and it puts me in a position to say that his knowledge of the subject is unique both in detail and in general, so that readers of the present volume may rest assured that facts and facts alone are dealt with in its pages.

H. W. Staner,
Editor of *The Autocar*,

Coventry,
October, 1914.

CHAPTER 1

The Scope of the Motor Vehicle

When we remember that the motor vehicle as we know it today, (1914), is the result of a development not more than a quarter of a century old, its enormous influence upon the character of modern warfare must indeed be regarded as remarkable. Especially is this so in view of the fact that progress has not in the main been dictated by military considerations, but almost entirely by the requirements of private individuals and of peaceful trading concerns. The case is very different from that of the aeroplane and the airship, which from the very moment that they began to appear as practical possibilities, were recognised as having far greater potentialities in connection with warfare than in any other sphere. The whole science of flight has been studied to a great extent from this point of view, and the Government Departments concerned, in all civilised countries, have recognised the necessity of keeping in touch with and encouraging the movement, and have realised all along the nature of the work to be done by the flying corps.

On the other hand, the use of the motor vehicle was extended in the first instance mainly as a sport, and as a new occupation for well-to-do individuals of a mechanical turn of mind. There is an attraction about speed in all forms, and consequently, it was on this point that attention was for many years concentrated. Furthermore, developments were influenced to no slight extent by changes of fashion, and the need of satisfying the requirements of people who were not necessarily qualified to direct progress into the best possible channels. The motor vehicle was used as a luxury, and exploited as a means of bringing into being new forms of sport, for many years before it acquired sufficient reliability or worked with sufficient economy to justify its employment on economic grounds.

The industrial motor industry is, in fact, at the present day, (1914), only about ten years old. In the first instance, one of the principal factors in securing the occasional use of motor vans was the advertisement value of a rather unusual type of vehicle, which naturally attracted considerable attention wherever it went. A little later mechanical transport was adopted by a limited number of firms, not on account of any superiority in economy or reliability over old systems of delivery, but rather with a view to extending the area embraced, and so gaining an advantage over competing concerns more than sufficient to balance the increased cost involved by the employment of vehicles by no means cheap either as regards first cost or operating expenses.

Once the industry was established, however, its rapid growth was inevitable, since it was found possible to construct vehicles the employment of which was more than justified on purely economic grounds. The line of least resistance was found in connection with public services and hackney carriages for the conveyance of passengers, while in the carriage of goods the new means of transport had to compete with cheap if slow systems of delivery by horsed vehicle, and with the railways which, if not offering a direct method, at least offered a very cheap one when a large volume of traffic had to be handled.

In the other sphere, competition was limited chiefly to the horsed 'bus, the horsed cab and the tram car, and the last named was under a disadvantage in some quarters, since conditions exist in parts of London and in various other cities extremely unfavourable to the complete employment of railed transport on the roads. The motor cab was assisted in driving the horse cab off the streets by the stupid conservatism of the old-fashioned cab driver, who refused point-blank to employ the taximeter, and so to forego the advantage which he had obtained by keeping his fare in a certain amount of ignorance as to the proper legal charges to which he was entitled. The promoters of the early motor-cab companies took advantage of this state of affairs, and introduced the motor cab and the taximeter simultaneously.

The vehicle itself had the attraction of novelty and the advantage of greater speed, while its early popularity was still more directly due to the taximeter giving an accurate check of the amount payable on every journey. In this sphere, consequently, the victory of mechanical over horse transport was rapid and inevitable. Simultaneously, the motor omnibus made steady, if not quite such speedy, progress. Its advantage in speed over the horse 'bus was at first the determining factor, but after improvements in the mechanism, giving increased comfort and reliability, it was able to get the better also of the electric tram in spite of the advantage possessed by the railed vehicle of larger carrying capacity, which of course tends towards reduced operating costs per passenger carried.

The inflexible nature of a tramway system has been the principal factor in securing the popularity of a free road vehicle, and at the present moment the motor omnibus is able to compete directly with great success against the electric tram car. So it came about that passenger transport was very rapidly converted to mechanical power. If London is taken as an example, we find that at the present moment over 95 *per cent*, of passenger transport is carried on by mechanical vehicles, while certainly not more than 15 *per cent*, of goods transport has yet been similarly diverted. Nevertheless, the motor vehicle for the carriage of goods has made great progress, particularly in this country.

Throughout its history, it has been greatly helped by the prior existence of the steam traction engine. From these heavy and slow machines, suitable only for limited use in particular spheres, have been developed two very useful classes of lighter steam-propelled machines coming under the provisions of the Motor Car Acts. The first is the steam tractor, which is merely a small edition of the traction engine, able, on account of its lighter weight, to travel at considerably higher speeds. The other is the steam lorry, which is an extremely valuable machine for the carriage of anything up to about six tons of goods at speeds of about five miles per hour. From the five-ton steam lorry there has more recently developed a lighter type of steam vehicle in the shape of the three-ton lorry, generally running on rubber tyres, and so entitled legally to travel at much higher speeds.

The great economy of steam motors made it absolutely necessary for the makers of internal combustion industrial vehicles to study every possibility of reducing operating costs. They had on their side advantages as regards higher speed possibilities and more complete independence of fuel supplies. The steam motor of ordinary type cannot be conveniently designed to carry with it fuel and water supplies adequate for very long journeys. On the other hand, the steamer has the great advantage of being able to exert tremendous power at low road speeds. The steam engine is more flexible and more capable of standing a heavy overload than the internal combustion engine. Even if it is brought almost to a standstill, it can go on applying the full steam pressure behind its piston during every stroke.

A GROUP OF MOTORS IN THE SERVICE OF THE FLYING CORPS AT A RECENT REVIEW IN FRANCE

Given adequate supplies of fuel and water, it is an admirable and very economical machine for all sorts of rough and heavy work. Curiously enough, the steam lorry and the steam tractor have been essentially British developments, and as such they have done much to bring the British industrial petrol vehicle up to its present high standard of perfection.

The essential differences between a tractor and a lorry should here be noted. The tractor is designed merely to haul a load, while the lorry is primarily intended to carry its load. In the first case, the engine and the load-carrying vehicle are two separate units coupled together; in the second, they form one unit. The latter is the more convenient arrangement so far as manoeuvring in enclosed spaces is concerned, since a good deal of skill is needed to back a tractor train with accuracy. Also, the steam lorry uses its load to increase the adhesive power of its driving wheels. On the other hand, the steam tractor can itself be doing useful work, while some of its load-carrying vehicles or trailers are being loaded or unloaded. By providing two sets of trailers, it can be kept usefully employed and need not waste time at its terminal points.

Moreover, if it is required to work under very difficult conditions, it is a great advantage to be able to unhitch the engine from the trailer. If, for example, the bed of a river has to be crossed and the wheels sink into loose sand, the tractor is unhitched and run through without its load until it reaches solid ground. When it is brought to a standstill, its engine is employed through the medium of wire rope gear to drag the loaded trailer slowly but very surely out of its difficulty. Thus, for cross-country work, the tractor has much to recommend it, and it is not surprising that the success of the five-ton steamer has led to systematic endeavours to perfect internal combustion tractors possessing all the same advantages, and also self-contained for long journeys as regards fuel and water supplies.

Mention has already been made of the fact that, when a tractor is used, the load does not assist the adhesion of the wheels. This constitutes, as it were, an artificial limit to the tractive power, and has naturally caused some designers to consider methods by which the engine power of a tractor could be applied not only to one pair of wheels but to all the wheels, so that the whole weight of the engine itself can be used to secure adhesion.

The four-wheel drive is not common in commercial service, as it has only been found necessary under a limited number of very severe conditions. A good deal has been done, however, in this direction, particularly in France. The resulting vehicle need not be purely a tractor. In fact, we often find heavy lorries employed not only to carry a substantial load, but to haul an additional lighter load in a trailer. As a rule, these trailers have iron-tyred wheels, but for service in which economy of engine power is more important than economy of money, rubber tyres are usually fitted, since they have the effect of reducing the power absorbed in hauling the trailer by about 25 *per cent*.

Another development which is due mainly to the difficulties of adopting the internal combustion engine for the haulage of heavy loads without shock, is the petrol-electric system. In this system the power of the car engine is used to drive an electric dynamo. This dynamo generates current which is either supplied direct to electric motors or else stored in a battery of accumulators, the former method being the better and more likely to survive. Sometimes one electric motor is used, taking the place of an ordinary gear box, and driving the back wheels through a universally jointed shaft and a differential gear. In other cases, two balanced electric motors are employed in or near the driving wheels. In others again, two motors are used, each driving through shaft and differential gear to one axle of the vehicle, and so providing an electric four-wheel drive.

Another arrangement is the provision of four electric motors, one for each wheel. The vehicle is controlled through the medium of a "controller;" that is to say, an apparatus which, by the movement of a handle, varies the electrical connections and so makes the installation suitable for providing either a big torque at low speeds, or a comparatively light torque at high speeds. Electrical machinery is also in a sense self-regulating, and consequently a well-designed petrol-electric transmission is tantamount to the provision of an infinitely variable change speed gear.

One of the strongest arguments against the petrol-electric method is that, when the machine is running fairly light and fast, the electrical machinery involves certain unnecessary power losses. Consequently, systems have been devised in which mechanical and electrical drive are combined, the latter only operating the vehicle under conditions equivalent to an increase of load on the engine.

Efforts have been made for many years past to evolve a satisfactory internal combustion engine using paraffin or some other heavy and comparatively cheap oil in place of petrol. While these attempts have by no means failed, the practical results are up to the present more or less limited to the use of paraffin fuel in tropical or semi-tropical countries, where the higher temperature facilitates its employment. Among the disadvantages of paraffin are difficulties in starting up, a tendency to soot up the sparking plugs, the need of more frequent cleaning of cylinders, and a certain amount of disagreeable smell, partly due to the creeping of the liquid through every available crevice.

So far as the ordinary petrol van or lorry is concerned, various types have been developed to meet a variety of commercial needs. A certain number of light vans are run on pneumatic tyres, but the solid tyre is preferred wherever economy is more important than speed. It of course goes without saying that, if a chassis is to run on solid tyres, it must be of substantial construction, and so designed that its mechanism will not be injured by the fact that the solid tyre is not so capable as the pneumatic of absorbing small vibrations.

A very popular type of motor van is designed to carry about 25 or 30 cwt. These machines are capable of speeds up to about 25 or even 30 miles per hour in emergency, and can average comfortably 14 to 16 miles. Under reasonable conditions, they can cover daily journeys of 100 to 120 miles. Among larger types the 3-tonner predominates. This class of machine can be generally used for daily journeys of 70 to 90 miles, averaging perhaps 11 or 12 miles per hour. It usually consumes petrol at the rate of about 1 gallon to 8 miles, though better results are obtainable under good conditions.

There are also a large number of 5-ton petrol lorries in commercial service. These can be advantageously used to cover 60 or 70 miles a day, consuming about 1 gallon of petrol to every 6 miles run. The motor cab runs about 20 to 25 miles on a gallon of petrol, and the motor omnibus about 7 to 10 miles. This question of fuel consumption is, of course, distinctly important in military service, when adequate supplies are only maintained at the right points with considerable difficulty.

In later chapters some account is given of the attempts made by various governments to influence the development of motor traction into the directions dictated by their military needs, but this brief sketch of the general trend of events will be sufficient to indicate the present position, and to provide the necessary knowledge for the appreciation of the facts and considerations to which we shall now turn.

CHAPTER 2

The Importance of the Military Motor

Although we, in Great Britain, have developed the industrial motor vehicle almost entirely with a view to the improvement of communications in time of peace, various circumstances, which will be referred to in more detail in a later chapter, have led other countries to fasten their attention more firmly on to the application of mechanical power to military needs. Very considerable sums of money have been expended during the past five or six years with this end in view, and such expenditure could only have been justified if a full study of the probable course of a great war under modern conditions had led to the conclusion that the motor is something more than an accessory and convenience, but is rather one of the prime essentials of success. In order to prove that this view is, in fact, held by those who have devoted their whole time to the study of modern warfare, one need go no further than the now famous or notorious book on *Germany and the Next War* by General F. von Bernhardi:

> In a future European war 'masses' will be employed to an extent unprecedented in any previous one. Weapons will be used whose deadliness will exceed all previous experience. More effective and varied means of communication will be available than were known in earlier wars. These three momentous factors will mark the war of the future.

From this statement it is clear that, even if only improvement in means of communication is considered, the motor vehicle forms one of the three greatest factors in moulding the course of modern warfare. Railways have been available in many previous wars, and there can be no doubt that the reference to more effective and varied means of communication is occasioned almost entirely by the development of motor vehicles suitable for use in the transport and supply columns. Simultaneously, both of the other prime factors are affected by the introduction of motor vehicles. Road motors can assist materially in massing men rapidly at any desired point, and mechanical power is absolutely essential for the transport of guns of enormous calibre, the employment of which in the field is only in this way rendered possible.

Quoting again from the same authority we get an idea of the bearing of our subject upon a military theory now universally accepted as true.

The commander who can carry out all operations quicker than the enemy, and can concentrate and employ greater masses in a narrow space than they can, will always be in a position to collect a numerically superior force in the decisive direction; if he controls the more effective troops he will gain decisive successes against one part of the hostile army, and will be able to exploit them against other divisions of it before the enemy can gain equivalent advantages in other parts of the field. . . . If the assailant can advance in the decisive direction with superior numbers, and can win the day, because the enemy cannot utilise his numerical superiority, there is a possibility of an ultimate victory over the arithmetically stronger army.

Taking this statement in conjunction with the well-known German theory that safety only lies in offensive warfare, we realise immediately the incalculable importance of the introduction of any new system which will give to large bodies of men the powers of more free and more rapid movement. When armies are increased beyond certain numerical limits, it becomes absolutely necessary for them to depend upon supplies brought up regularly from the rear, and not upon the uncertainties of living upon the country.

Improved means of communication facilitate the handling and feeding of large masses, but tie them down to railway systems and main roads, and must, if they fail or break down in the course of a campaign, aggravate the difficulties, because the troops were accustomed to their use, and the commanders counted upon them.

We have here a complete recognition of two most important points. The first is, that the use of motors in the transport and supply columns, if successfully carried on, represents an enormous advantage, which may even allow ultimate victory to come to a numerically inferior army. In the second place, we have the acknowledgment that any breakdown in the service for which the motor vehicles are responsible, will be fatal to success.

A military correspondent of the *Daily Telegraph* has recently emphasised the same point. He has pointed out that hitherto the massing of an army of about a quarter of a million men has represented the probable limit of possibilities, and that even then such numbers could only be massed for a short period. The Russo-Japanese war, in which larger numbers were engaged, has by no means disproved this theory, since it partook of the nature of a siege rather than that of a field campaign. At the present moment, the enormous numbers dealt with involve certain limitations in movement, the scope of which is dictated by the distribution of railways and of roads. Without motor transport, the rate of movement of huge armies would be necessarily very slow, the radius of action from railhead would be small, and the daily movement of the troops would be strictly circumscribed for more reasons than one.

The effect of the introduction of motor transport is somewhat similar to that which would be obtained if the railway could, in a few hours, be extended in any direction along any made road for a distance of about forty or fifty miles. The delivery of supplies, as it were in retail, to the troops must still be carried out by horse transport, since motor lorries are not suitable for continuous use where made roads do not exist. The comparatively slow movement of horsed vehicles even now affects the rate of progress of an army. When huge bodies of men are in motion, the depth from the front to the rear of the army is very considerable, and at the end of the day the supplies have to be brought up from the rear to the front in time to enable the whole force to be fed.

The use of transport and supply motors does not amount merely to the employment of a large number of these machines for miscellaneous duties, but rather corresponds to bringing into existence a new, link in the chain of the main system of supply. The existence of railways behind the army is assumed. At some safe point along the railway is formed the base, and from this base stores are brought up to a point known as "railhead." This is the point where, for the time

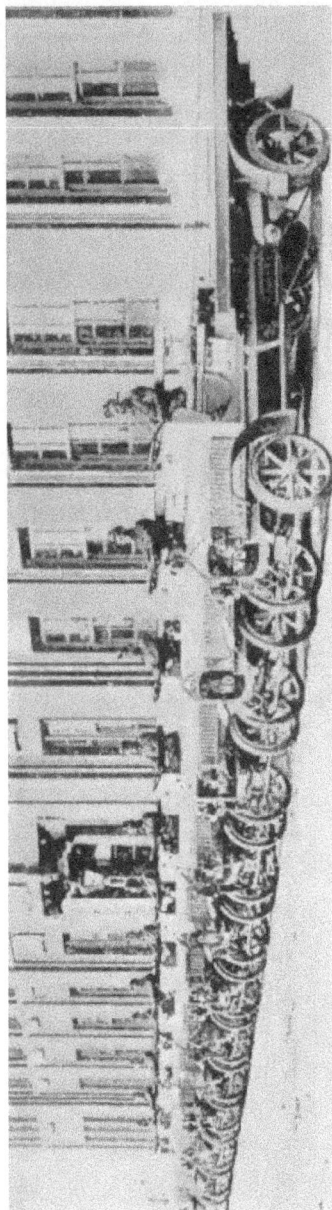

PART OF BIG FLEET OF "ALBION" LORRIES PURCHASED BY THE BRITISH WAR OFFICE

A GROUP OF BRITISH "BERNA" LORRIES TAKEN OVER BY THE WAR DEPARTMENT

being, military rail traffic ceases. It is evident that railhead is a variable quantity, liable to move forward or backward from day to day. The main accumulation of stores is at the base, and the stock at railhead at any moment consists only of sufficient to meet one day's requirements. Before the introduction of motor transport, the whole of the supplies from railhead had to be taken by horsed vehicle, and subsequently distributed in the same way among the troops. Under the new method, motor lorries carry the supplies up to a place called "refilling point," which is a movable point situated from day to day in the most convenient position possible to arrange, with a view to the distribution of supplies by horsed vehicle to the army.

In the old system, the transport vehicles worked in *echelons*. The first of these, with the baggage and supplies for a day, followed so closely behind the troops as to be able to join them every night. The next, half a day's march behind, carried supplies sufficient to replenish the first column daily. Further back again were other *echelons* carrying on the same scheme. This meant that the whole of the roads for enormous distances behind the forces were encumbered by transport. Between railhead and the army there were many links involving endless possibilities of confusion, and consequently shortage in supplies. Moreover, food came up to the troops very slowly from the base, and it was impossible to supply a regular stock of fresh meat and bread.

The advantage of the new system is based on the speed capacity of the motor vehicle, a supplementary point being an enormous reduction in the length of a column carrying a given quantity of supplies. It is, however, the higher speed of the motor which has the greatest effect, since it enables many columns to be replaced by one. In the words of Colonel Paul:

> One *echelon* of mechanical transport can do the work of five *echelons* of horse transport, and one column will suffice to connect the horse transport immediately behind the troops with the railway.

The result is to facilitate operations of troops up to a distance from railhead represented by half of a full day's work for the motors. The simplest way of appreciating the result obtained is to take an actual example. Under the new system, on, let us say, Tuesday evening, the soldier at the front is provided with a hot meal of fresh meat, cooked by the regimental travelling kitchens on the march. This food had been handed over to the kitchens on Monday evening by the

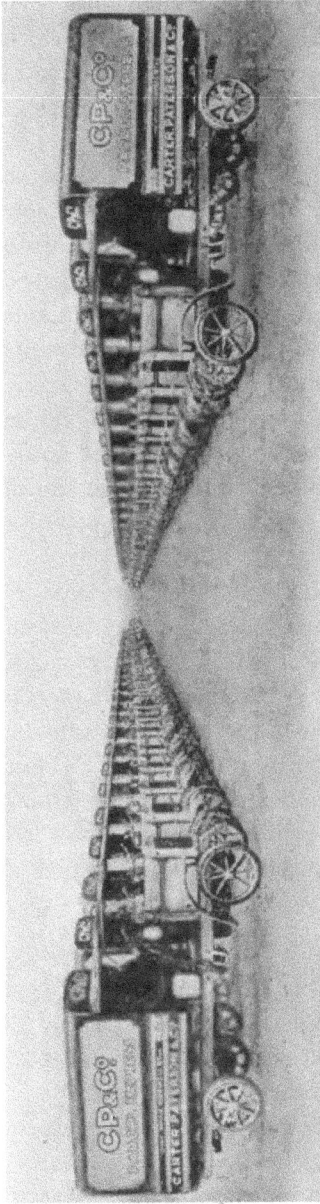

A FLEET OF "THORNYCROFT" LORRIES REQUISITIONED FOR SERVICE.

A FLEET OF "HALLFORD" LORRIES CALLED UP IMMEDIATELY ON THE OUTBREAK OF WAR.

distributing horsed vehicles, which had received it sometime during Monday at the refilling point a few miles back from the motor supply column, which had left railhead perhaps 50 miles from the front in the small hours of Monday morning. Previously, the supplies had been brought down by rail from the base, and in this way the food which the soldiers are eating on Tuesday night, was probably to be found in the neighbourhood of the base on Sunday afternoon in the shape of live animals.

Working out the scheme from a rather different point of view, the soldier on the Tuesday night is in possession of Wednesday's supply of bread and cheese, and an emergency ration of preserved meat in case of any delays or breakdown in the transport service. The horsed vehicles are at the time empty, and are returning to meet the motors at refilling point. The motors by this time are back at railhead waiting for Wednesday's supplies to be discharged from the railway trains. At about three o'clock on Wednesday morning the motors will be loaded and ready to start. Their speed capacity will enable them easily to catch up with the distributing horsed vehicles before the end of Wednesday's march, and to tranship their supplies at refilling point for distribution on Wednesday evening.

The whole system is, in reality, very simple, and it enables large armies in the field to be supplied daily with fresh meat and bread instead of being dependent on food brought up slowly and in many stages, and for that reason necessarily of a character less nutritious, and much more liable in the long run to cause illness among the men. At the same time, the big carrying capacity of the motor has served to clear the roads behind the army of an enormous block of vehicles essential in the past, but now no longer necessary. In connection with this point, Colonel R. H. Ewart, D.S.O., representing the Indian Office at the Imperial Motor Transport Conference of 1913, gave some very interesting figures, which may be quoted as an extreme case:

> Up to 1910 the reports show that there were nearly five and a half million bullock carts in British India alone, and in all our wars up to date, we have had to mobilise a very large number of these carts for our line of communication work. We find that when moving in large bodies, the utmost speed we can rely upon is about one-and-a-half miles an hour. We have worked out that it takes six bullock carts to move in eighty days what one 2-ton lorry can transport in ten. The bullock carts take up

twice the room on the road for a given load, and in the matter of establishment—a question which you will all realise in the time of war is a very serious one—it takes thirty-five men, drivers, artificers and supervisors to look after what one man could do with a lorry.

From these figures it will be seen what an enormous saving is effected by the use of motors, even if we only take the point of view of the feeding, maintenance and payment of the men actually employed in the transport columns themselves.

The impossibility of imposing upon horsed vehicles the necessity for gaining fifty or even thirty miles in the course of a day, in order to catch up by the evening with an advancing army after leaving railhead in the morning, is perfectly obvious. The truth of the statement already made that the use of motors for transport and supply work is a necessity and not merely a convenience in modern warfare, is thus made clear, and under the circumstances, readers who are perhaps more attracted by the more showy, but less essential, uses of motors in war, will understand that a consideration of the subject of this book must necessarily be devoted very largely to the organisation and *matériel* of the supply columns.

The class of vehicle most commonly favoured for the work of feeding troops in the field is the 3-ton petrol lorry, capable of covering eighty or ninety miles in a day, and if need be of travelling under fairly favourable conditions at twenty miles an hour. Behind very mobile troops, such as cavalry, preference is sometimes given to lighter lorries rated to carry 30 cwt. or 2 tons, and capable of rather higher rates of speed and rather bigger daily mileages. Some European Powers favour for general work lorries carrying 4 or 5 tons, and in addition capable of drawing an extra 2 tons or so upon a trailer. In every case, the internal combustion vehicle is preferred on account of its independence upon frequent renewals of fuel and water supplies. However, steam tractors are often used for various classes of specially heavy work, as, for example, for drawing the travelling workshops which have to be established at the movable base of the supply columns at railhead.

CHAPTER 3

Trials and Manoeuvres

Naturally, the motor vehicle could not be entrusted with work of the first importance in time of war without previously going through a period of encouragement and probation. Some fourteen years ago, motor cars and cycles began to be used in small numbers during military manoeuvres in Great Britain and elsewhere.

In the French manoeuvres of 1901, cars and motor tricycles were employed for transporting staff officers, and for scouting work. The motorists who lent the cars were entrusted with the duty of driving them, and were granted certain privileges on that account. Results were on the whole satisfactory.

In the same year, the British War Office, as a result of experience gained in South Africa, were encouraged to conduct trials of motor lorries. The entrants were five in number. Four of these were steam lorries, the makes represented being the Foden, Straker, and two types of Thornycroft. There was only one entrant of an internal combustion engined machine. This was a Milnes-Daimler modelled on the German Daimler cars, and having a four-cylinder engine rated at 25 h.p., with ignition by low-tension magneto. Fuel was supplied by pressure of the exhaust, and the car had a channel steel frame and large built-up steel wheels. Even at that comparatively early date, the Foden lorry was, in general appearance, very similar to the standard steam lorry of today, (1914).

It was, of course, fitted with a locomotive-type boiler, this being a practice which has since been adopted by almost all manufacturers of this class of machine. The Thornycroft lorries had vertical boilers, and the one type was representative of standard practice, the other being rather a peculiar machine driven from the rear. The Foden and standard Thornycroft were most successful in carrying out the very arduous road tests imposed, which involved a large number of particularly steep hills. The Foden was by far the most economical in water and fuel. The trials ended by cross-country tests in the Long Valley at Aldershot, and during these the Foden was unfortunately driven by accident into a deep ditch, with the result that its front axle was broken. Consequently, the standard Thornycroft received the first award and the benefit of subsequent small orders from the War Department, although at the time there was a rather strong feeling that the Foden ought also to have been recognised.

It was not until about two years later that, in the publication of evidence given before the commission appointed to inquire into the conduct of the South African war, the opinion of Lord Kitchener on the utility of motor transport in its then state of development was made public His views were expressed as follows:

We had (in South Africa) about forty-five steam road transport trains. As a rule they did useful work, but questions of weather, roads, water and coal distinctly limited their employment as compared with animal transport, to which they can only be regarded as supplementary. The motor lorries sent to South Africa did well. Thornycrofts are the best. They will in the future be found superior to steam road trains as field transport.

From this it will be seen that the main result of South African experience was to indicate the superiority of the comparatively light self-contained motor vehicle over the heavy traction engine.

In 1903, a considerable number of cars and cycles supplied by members of the Motor Volunteer Corps were used in the British manoeuvres. The cars employed numbered forty-three, and averaged about 12 h.p. They were used mainly for staff were not very successful. Some thirty motor cycles were employed for carrying despatches, and behaved on the whole splendidly. Mr. J. F. Ochs, in describing, during a lecture at the Royal Automobile Club, the results obtained, made a somewhat prophetic statement in his remark that, "If Mr. Marconi could perfect his invention, how useful a car fitted with it would be."

While the undoubted utility of motors for staff work and for scouting was recognised at least as a certainty of the future, progress in comparatively heavy military transport was for some years after this limited. The military authorities were averse to the use of petrol-driven cars, on account of the supposed danger of employing so inflammable a fuel. Efforts were made to use paraffin, but results were not particularly satisfactory. The Mechanical Transport Companies at Aldershot went on experimenting with and developing the use of steam vehicles, and particularly of steam tractors, which came to be regarded as, on the whole, more suitable for rough work than self-contained lorries. By 1906, the mechanical transport sections were in possession of adequate tractor-drawn workshops, to support the: varied fleet of mechanical vehicles available for a variety of purposes, as well as the staff cars, a limited number of which had been purchased by the War Department.

Arrangements had also been made for giving the drivers and mechanics some theoretical as well as practical knowledge, and the movement had in fact formed itself into the nucleus of what it was then supposed would be required; namely, an organisation providing for military service a large number of 5-ton steam tractors, and a limited number of cars and motor cycles for staff and scouting duty.

For some time, efforts to procure for army service some really reliable internal combustion tractors running on paraffin were continued. In February, 1909, trials were held at Aldershot, in connection with which a considerable premium and valuable prospective orders were offered as an inducement to manufacturers to turn their attention to this class of machine. The entrants, however, only numbered three. One of these was a substantial four-cylinder Thornycroft paraffin tractor, which performed well throughout and was ultimately successful in obtaining an award, though it does not appear that the type has since been adopted in any quantity. A very singular machine which did wonderful work for its power was a Broom and Wade single-cylinder paraffin tractor of about 20 h.p.

The work of hauling a heavy military trailer with a load of about 6 tons was, on occasions, too much for this machine under the sometimes very arduous conditions under which the trials were carried out. The third entry hardly came within the scope of what the War Department wished to encourage. It was a Stewart-Crosbie steam tractor with a two-cylinder compound double-acting engine giving 40 b.h.p. at 600 r.p.m. It was able to meet the stipulations as to capacity for carrying fuel and water supplies, since the boiler was of the vertical central-fired water-tube type working at 200 lbs. pressure, and supplying to the engine superheated steam which had been passed through coiled tubes in the furnace.

During the greater part of the trials the roads round Aldershot were covered with a thick coating of snow, which constituted a serious difficulty for iron-tyred tractors when using public thoroughfares in time of peace. In emergency, it would of course have been possible to fit spikes, or grips of some kind, to the wheels to prevent skidding and slipping, but this could only be done at the risk of great injury to the roads which did not appear justifiable under the circumstances. All three tractors were provided with means for employing their engine power through the medium of a wire rope, and this had to be utilised in some cases to get the loads up some of the very steep gradients encountered.

The trials terminated in an extraordinarily difficult test across the Long Valley. Here much loose sand was negotiated successfully, and afterwards the engines were required to get their loads across a deep swamp. The Thornycroft was the most successful, but even the little Broom & Wade machine managed to carry out the work by means of a system of pulleys applied to its wire rope gear. It was curious to watch this little engine dragging its big load in a trailer which had sunk almost to the wheel tops in mud and water. Occasionally, turf and mud had to be dug away from the front of the trailer, and when it was in motion the wheels were actually rotating slowly in the wrong direction under the influence of the pressure of a continuous supply of weed-bound mud surging over their tops.

These trials, if not satisfactory in attaining their main object, at least helped to demonstrate that practically nothing is impossible to a soundly constructed motor vehicle, if properly equipped for rough work. Intermittently, experiments have been made at Aldershot with various machines of more or less peculiar construction. Among these may be remembered the Pedrail tractor, the wheels of which carry a number of articulated feet which, as the machine progresses, plant themselves one after another squarely upon the ground.

The necessary mechanism was, however, too complex to render anything of the sort suitable for extensive military use, and the same trouble probably applies to the Caterpillar type of tractor, in which the wheels are surrounded by a track in the form of a sort of endless chain, which lays itself as the machine moves upon the ground, and distributes the weight over a large area. Passing over rough country, a tractor of this sort rolls like a ship at sea, but is very seldom in any real difficulty, even when traversing ditches or fairly low hedges. Steering has to be effected by allowing the wheels on one side to over-run those upon the other, with the result that the engine turns with a sort of skidding motion.

An interesting test of the value of the motor car in war was carried out by the Automobile Association on March 17th, 1909. The Association made an offer to Lord Haldane, then Secretary of State for War, to transport a battalion by motor vehicles to any coast town that the War Office might consider a possible scene of invasion. The point ultimately selected was Hastings. For the purpose of the scheme it was assumed that a sudden concentration of troops at Hastings had become necessary, and that a battalion of the Guards was about to entrain in London, when information was received that a portion of the railway line had been destroyed by spies or agents working on behalf of the enemy. Under such circumstances, the battalion could only be sent by road. On the date named, a battalion of infantry at full war strength, over 1,000 officers and men, with machine guns, ammunition, medical stores, tools, food, water, baggage, blankets, and other impedimenta amounting to some 30 tons, was distributed among 286 touring cars and about 50 motor lorries.

The cars were lent and driven by members of the Automobile Association, and several manufacturers of heavy motor vehicles provided the necessary number of lorries for carrying the guns and stores.

The battalion was a composite one, consisting of officers and men of the Grenadier and Scots Guards from Chelsea Barracks, Wellington Barracks, and the Tower. The programme, which entailed picking up the men at their respective barracks, joining up the three columns at the Crystal Palace at 10 a.m. and arriving at Hastings soon after 1 p.m. was carried through successfully, and within half an hour of arrival the battalion with its full equipment was marched along the seafront.

The experiment aroused considerable interest in military circles in this country and abroad, particularly so in Germany, where a number of newspapers published full particulars and a plan of the route taken.

In 1908 the German Army Department adopted the scheme which it has since enforced for securing military transport, and from that time onwards annual trials have been held, generally in the late autumn, and over heavy and mountainous roads. In this they have differed from the majority of the annual trials held in France, first of all under the auspices of the Automobile Club of France, and later directly by the military authorities. Our neighbours have shown a tendency to make the routes selected somewhat easy, and not to test the vehicles over unduly severe gradients. The German scheme was reconsidered at the end of 1912 as a result of the experience obtained up to that time.

The trials of 1912 were over a distance of about 1,300 miles, including roads through the mountains of central Germany. The distance covered each day by the 4-ton lorries drawing additional 2-ton loads on trailers was about 60 miles. Subsequently, the newer regulations prescribed more strict limits of axle weight, in view of uncertainty as to the strength of the roads and bridges which would have to be negotiated. A minimum engine power of 35 h.p. was prescribed, and gradients of one in seven had to be taken with full load and equipment. An interesting point of the new German regulations is the provision of a belt pulley somewhere on the driving shaft for the purpose of operating machine tools. Another point is the stipulation that the brakes of the trailing vehicle shall be capable of being operated from the driving seat of the lorry. A certain degree of standardisation was at the same time introduced.

In the same year, a big step towards the proper utilisation of motor transport for military work was taken by an extensive experiment made in this direction during the British Army manoeuvres. The use of mechanical transport was subsequently referred to by the king as one of the special features on that occasion, and the opinion was very generally expressed that the rather sudden and early termination of the manoeuvres was due to the unexpected effect of motor transport in increasing the mobility of the troops, and bringing the opposing forces into contact with one another with startling rapidity. Even so late as 1912, a certain number of military authorities were still very doubtful as to the advisability of relying on the motor vehicle in active service, but the manoeuvres in question undoubtedly proved the case, although the difficulties of operating mechanical transport for the first time on an extensive scale were increased by the fact that the machines available were of all sorts of makes and types, no attempts at standardisation having been possible.

Many of the machines hired for the occasion were in very poor condition, and did not compare favourably with those owned by the government. Consequently, the difficulties of working in convoy at short intervals were accentuated. All the motor transport was concentrated on one side, and the armies dependent upon it were kept well supplied daily with fresh meat, the opposing forces being dependent on horsed transport and chilled meat. Motor buses were on one or two occasions during the manoeuvres utilised with great success for the rapid movement of fairly large bodies of men. These manoeuvres probably represented the last appearance of traction engines for any military use other than the haulage of very heavy guns, or other kinds of quite abnormal work, not forming any part of the regular system of supply and transport.

During the last few years, (as at time of first publication), trials have been held at irregular intervals by the War Department far the purpose of testing the suitability of various specially constructed motor lorries for recognition under the subsidy scheme, the nature of which is explained in detail in a later chapter. The last trials of this kind took place early in 1914. An official report published in June stated that results had been very successful as regards both the number of entrants, and the general standard of excellence of the vehicles submitted.

The average speeds both on easy and on hilly routes were well above those specified. Radiators were found to be amply large to be effective even in the hottest weather. The Mechanical Transport Committee reiterated their opinion that one of the two systems of brakes should act upon the propeller shaft. The average fuel consumption of the competing cars was exceedingly good, working out at 52 gross ton miles per gallon. The best result was about 63 gross ton miles per gallon over a distance of about 200 miles. On the whole, it is evident that the cars were very satisfactory, since it was stated that there appeared to be no necessity to make any serious alterations in specifying for future requirements.

The most recent French trials were hardly completed when war broke out. They were as usual well patronised, but not calculated on the whole to try the machines to the utmost. It was intended in subsequent years to introduce new and more stringent regulations, but the opinion was fairly generally expressed among manufacturers that the government in doing so were differentiating their own needs too far from ordinary business requirements, and that it would be impossible to find a market for the types indicated. Early in the year, another series of trials of considerable importance was held in France, for the purpose of testing new types of four-wheel driven tractors. These machines are needed particularly for the haulage of artillery, and further reference to them will therefore be deferred until that subject comes up for consideration

CHAPTER 4

Experiences of Motors in Active Service

Although mechanical transport was employed during the South African war, the experiences then gained must not be applied with too much rigidity to the conditions of the conflict taking place in Europe. In South Africa, a considerable number of traction engines were put into service, while steam motor lorries were also used. Colonel R. E. Crompton, C.B., who was in charge of the British transport columns, has described how:

> De Wet, knowing the country, destroyed bridge after bridge until the roads and the railways were only islands, disconnected by things called 'deviations'—horrible places, full of dead animals, horse transport, animal transport of all kinds, which had died there, simply because there was practically no road....The fact that we were able, even though we had broken engines, to repair them from our spares, so that the dead engines became live engines, so impressed Lord Roberts that he felt that we were at the birth of real, practical mechanical military transport with all the advantages it gives.

There can be no doubt that the experience obtained during the South African war pointed directly to the use in the first case of steam tractors, and later—when they could be sufficiently perfected—of internal combustion tractors with a bigger radius of action. These conclusions resulted not only from the inherent conditions of military service, but also from the local conditions of the country in which this particular war took place.

Reviewing the possibilities of South Africa in times of peace, Mr.

W. W. Hoy, the General Manager of the Government Railways and Harbours, while approving of the use of light passenger and goods vehicles up to 2 or 3 tons capacity, lays stress on the desirability of the light paraffin tractor for easy services on good roads, and the heavy paraffin tractor for cross-country work with trains of trailers each carrying from 12 to 25 tons of goods. If we admit that a country in which these represent the main normal requirement cannot be safely taken as indicating accurately even the war requirements of other countries, we are reduced for practical experience to the Italian campaign in Tripoli and the recent wars in the Balkans. Italy is one of those countries in which commercial motor transport has not, owing to unfavourable local conditions, made any great progress.

As a result the war was begun without any provision having been made in this direction, and the authorities were at first very sceptical as regards the desirability of employing motors at all in connection with the operations of the army. After much discussion, two light lorries, fitted with twin pneumatic tyres on the back wheels, were sent out on trial. These served very rapidly to convince the staff officers of the superiority of the system over horse transport. Consequently, thirty more light Fiat lorries were sent out as promptly as possible, and these were followed by larger consignments, bringing the whole fleet in use up to the number of about 200.

Arrived at Tripoli, the cars were slung off the transport ships on to big pontoons, and towed to the quay. From that point they were immediately employed for the transport of all kinds of war material, as well as provisions and forage. They were further utilised for the conveyance of large bodies of troops to the front, and for carrying wounded to the hospitals and dead to the improvised cemeteries. Most of the country over which they operated was entirely devoid of roads, and consisted chiefly of rough loose desert strewn with rocks and treacherous sandy hills. These peculiar conditions account for the type of vehicle selected for employment. Heavier lorries on solid tyres would no doubt have experienced even greater difficulties in negotiating country of this class.

The following extract, from a full account published by the manufacturers of the uses to which their vehicles were put, will serve to give an idea of the varied employment of military motors:

At the Battle of Zanzur, on June 8th, 1912, fifty-four vehicles took part and were divided into four columns under the personal command of Capt. Corazzi. Ten were under the command of an officer at the disposal of the Medical Corps; a second column, under the command of Lieut. Milani, carried a load of barbed wire and netting, sand bags and shovels; a third column, in Lieut. Bosio's charge, carried also 800 spades, 600 shovels, sand bags, and barbed wire; and a fourth column of fourteen lorries, under Lieut. Marocco, took a large quantity of dynamite and other explosives in addition to pioneers' tools.

The first column to move were the ambulances, which left Tripoli at two o'clock, and at 3.30 came out of the outer redoubt at Gargaresh to follow the fighting column and to work under the instructions of a surgeon-captain. The other columns left Tripoli about three o'clock, and at 4.15 at Gargaresh, about 5½ miles from Tripoli, they formed up in a square about 350 yards in front of the redoubt under cover of a hill, waiting for orders. At 5.30 they advanced, and leaving cover of the hills, moved forward about 2½ miles beyond the batteries.

The nature of the ground changed as the columns approached a sandbank, which had until then protected them from the enemy's fire. The passage over this sand dune was extremely difficult, as the cars had to proceed in single file at walking pace, exposed to a violent rifle fire. Proceeding round the extreme north of the Arabo-Turkish trenches the columns reached the Marabotto of Abd-el-Gelil shortly after the arrival of the third battalion of the Fortieth Fusiliers, mountain artillery, and a company of pioneers, and proceeded with the work of fortification. When the columns returned to Gargaresh, and while the Rainaldi Brigade was engaged against overwhelming forces of the enemy, one of the motor columns, acting under Lieut. Milani, was ordered to load provisions, whilst the other two were told off to join the ambulance section. In the very line of fire the motors brought succour to the wounded, conveyed some seventy disabled soldiers to the temporary hospital at Gargaresh, and carried forty dead to the cemetery.

At Gargaresh the order arrived to convey to Marabut the provisions and luggage of the 6th and 40th regiments of the line. The three motor columns therefore re-formed, one going to Tripoli to load provisions and returning to Marabut, the other two being loaded up with luggage. The three columns then returned to Tripoli.

After two years of incessant service, and notwithstanding the "emery" effect of the fine sand which was carried in clouds by the wind and penetrated everywhere, it is generally understood that the Italian military motor fleet maintained reliable services throughout the war, and that the individual machines were in surprisingly good condition when their service was completed. Results were, at any rate, sufficiently satisfactory to justify the Italian Government in placing considerable further orders, with a view to increasing their motor columns. This war was probably the first event which enabled the motor vehicle to prove itself in practice absolutely essential as a military implement. A Tripoli newspaper summed up the value of the experience obtained:

> Many people will have asked themselves how it was possible for the Lequio Division to live, march, fight, and win with a base of operations distant from 70 to 200 miles, with rapid and long deviations which were almost of daily occurrence, in a country so barren and inhospitable that man and beast would perish if they were left for only two or three days without provisions.
>
> The motor lorry provided the solution of the problem; by its use in a few hours provisions were brought from the stores and bases to the fighting column, having been conveyed possibly hundreds of miles, and, further, by its means not one day passed without the troops having bread, wine, and coffee. The motor lorry was ubiquitous; it transported ammunition or succoured the wounded, fetched fodder for the horses and other animals, or money for the troops and for the Arabs; it brought new boots for the soldiers or delivered urgent messages, as well as being used for the transport of troops from the various bases right up to the first fighting line in battle. Only the advent of the autocar rendered possible many of the daring moves of this war, as it solved the difficulties of desert transport.

As regards the uses of motors during the various Balkan campaigns, the only reliable and available information appears to be that contained in a series of articles contributed by Capt. A. H. Trapmann of the *Daily Telegraph* to the columns of Motor Traction. At the commencement of the war in 1912, there were less than 100 motor vehicles in Greece, and some sixty of these—the property of Greek subjects—*were* immediately commandeered. The machines formed a fleet very far from ideal, representing cars of all makes and sizes, many of them suffering from negligent treatment or unskilful handling, and some very near the termination of a chequered career.

The officers entrusted with the duty of purchasing the machines were completely ignorant of their value or qualities, and the drivers into whose hands they were subsequently put consisted mainly of people who could, or said they could, drive a motor car, though the great majority did not profess to possess any knowledge over and above that required for travelling with reasonable safety and certainty, assuming the mechanism of the cars to give no trouble at all. The better machines were chiefly allotted to the various generals and their staff officers, while some of the worst were fitted up with lorry bodies for the transport of goods.

After the fall of Salonica, the Greek objective was Janina, connected with the port of Preveza by an excellent road about sixty-three miles long. Directly Preveza fell into Greek hands, the authorities were faced with the problem of provisioning an army, in the first instance consisting of 15,000 men and gradually augmented to 60,000, operating against a fortified town in a totally barren country intersected by huge mountain ranges. The front of the army extended for about a hundred miles, and only one good road was available from the base to the centre of the advanced positions. Under these conditions, the authorities realised the possibilities of motor transport, and about thirty motor lorries, mainly obtained from Italy, were shipped to Preveza and put into service. It was found that each lorry could, in three hours, carry to the front about enough food for 1,000 men.

This, however, was not the only problem. The army was absorbing on the average one ton of ammunition per day for every thousand men. The lorries were only capable at the best of handling 2-ton loads, and consequently were kept more than fully occupied. Moreover, the road, though good in certain portions, was in others particularly dangerous, being very winding and hewn for the most part out of the side of a precipice. Heavy traffic and heavy rains contributed to make the conditions yet worse, and under the circumstances, it is not surprising that very serious accidents occurred, and that by the end of the first six weeks only nine out of the original thirty lorries were still upon the road. It then became necessary to replenish the supply, which was managed in one way or another, and the service was maintained with enormous difficulty under conditions of false economy, which dictated considerable purchases of unreliable second-hand machines. Even so, the results served completely to convince Captain Trapmann that motor transport was the only solution of the supply problem in warfare.

It seems that a similar opinion was forced upon the Greek military authorities, since one of the first moves when the second campaign became inevitable in 1913, was the purchase of one hundred motor lorries. This step, while good in itself, was inadequate, since no real provision was made for the supply of competent and responsible drivers, for adequate supervision, or for completely equipped workshops. Many of the drivers were well-to-do enthusiasts who had volunteered for service, and who very soon came to regret that they had done so. It is one thing to drive a good touring car and to fall back upon professional assistance whenever trouble occurs, but quite another to handle and maintain a heavy motor lorry without competent backing and under thoroughly bad conditions of service. Some 50 *per cent*, of the motor fleet was usually out of commission, and the staff of the repair shops were so incompetent that it was seldom that a car once taken to pieces was ever fit for the road again. The following extract from Capt. Trapmann's account gives some idea of the difficulties which had to be overcome:

"The strategy and tactics of the campaign against Bulgaria landed the Greek headquarters at Doyrani on July 8th, and there nearly two-thirds of the Greek motor service was concentrated on July 10th. Greek headquarters decided to move sixty miles west to Hadji Beylik along the railway, and the vital question was how the cars for the service of the staff, and the lorries for the army service were to accomplish the journey. The single-line railway track was impossible on account of unbridged gaps, and also because the railway was in urgent demand for transport. The only semblance of a road was a mule track two feet wide, which led for the most part through a tangle of vegetation, and occasionally amidst a wilderness of rocks and stones.

Eventually it was decided literally to force a road by sheer weight. The lorries took turns at leading, raced full speed for twenty yards, and then bashed their way through the jungle. After fifty yards or less the lorry would be brought to a standstill by the accumulation of rubbish piled up in front. This would be cleared away, the car would back, then start on a fresh charge. When a lorry got seriously damaged it would be replaced by another and taken in tow by a third. Sometimes explosives had to be used, and small rivers were bridged by the simple expedient of placing tree trunks in them until a car could cross. It was bumpy work.

In Macedonia a road of any sort was a luxury, the best roads could not compare as regards surface with a fourth-class English roadway, whilst as often as not the motors had to make their own road as they went along. It must be remembered, also, that driving in war time is very different from under peace conditions. Bridges and culverts have usually been destroyed, telegraph lines sag across the road, and at night time are apt to get entangled in the driver's neck with dire results. I, myself, have seen a goodly number of motor smashes, one when a temporary bridge gave way under an overloaded lorry, another when a contact mine exploded.

The worst accident I remember, however, took place soon after the fall of Janina. A very old and depreciated lorry was being used to convey passengers down to Preveza, a distance of sixty-three miles, by a mountain road which for half its length was cut on the edge of a precipice. At one of the awkward places on the road the steering gear broke, and the car with its human freight dashed over the cliff and fell into the river.

The conclusions reached by Captain Trapmann as a result of very exceptional opportunities of observing military motor transport under active service conditions should be of considerable value. His catalogue of desirable features is as follows:

(1) Clearance from ground in order to enable a car to pass over rock-strewn stretches.

(2) An adjustable cow-catcher in front for use at night on good stretches of road, on which, however, dead or wounded horses or men may be lying.

(3) An inclined bullet shield of light steel to protect the front of the radiator from casual sniping.

(4) A stout iron hook or ring in front and behind for towing purposes, especially when a river has to be negotiated, the bridge over which has been destroyed.

(5) Solid tyres with a set of non-skid chains which can be fitted when occasion arises.

(6) A wire grappler to preserve the driver from the danger of sagging telegraph wires hanging across the road. While the experiences detailed in this chapter are, comparatively speaking, on a very small scale, and consequently results cannot confi-

dently be applied in anticipation to a war of immensely greater magnitude, they have at least served to show that even unavoidable lack of experience, or avoidable lack of competence, cannot prevent the motor vehicle from being a very valuable asset behind an army in the field. The Tripoli and Balkan campaigns proved not only the necessity of employing motors for the work of the transport and supply columns, but also the possibility in so doing of saving the lives of very many wounded men who, when dependence was placed on slower methods, frequently died from exposure on their way down from the front to the base.

CHAPTER 5

Motor Ambulance Work

Among military uses of motor vehicles, the motor ambulance probably comes next in order of importance after the transport and supply waggons. Evidently with the motor ambulance must be grouped cars suitable for use in carrying wounded men who are not obliged to be transported in a recumbent position, and even ordinary touring cars when employed, as they are being somewhat extensively at the present moment, for taking convalescent men on health-giving motor trips. This last is a quite useful class of work in which even those motorists can participate who are only able to offer their services and those of their cars in the vicinity of their own homes and at specified hours.

In times of peace, the motor ambulance proper is, so far as its chassis is concerned, more akin to an industrial vehicle than to a touring car. The heavier examples, in some cases, run on solid rubber tyres, and in others on twin pneumatics, while the lighter types are fitted with single pneumatics of heavy section. In detail, the chassis is simple and strong, and well adapted to be put under the charge of a driver of only average mechanical ability. The principal points are that the vehicles should be silent in running, not liable to derangement and extremely well sprung. Owing to the first consideration, worm-driven chassis are particularly suitable for this class of work, and owing to the second a slightly modified light van chassis is generally to be preferred to the highly-refined but more complicated touring car.

In time of war, the ambulance chassis is, roughly speaking, anything big enough and sufficiently reliable that can be made available. For example, motor omnibuses can be without much difficulty adapted to this class of work, while touring cars are often quite suitable. The qualifications in the latter instance are fairly ample engine power, thorough reliability and strength for working over rough road sur-

AMBULANCE DRILL OF THE CITY OF LONDON BRANCH OF THE
BRITISH RED CROSS SOCIETY, USING CARS FITTED WITH THE
B.H.S. SPRING STRETCHER-SUSPENSION.
LIFTING THE STRETCHER.

LOADING THE STRETCHER INTO THE CAR BODY. IT IS AFTER-
WARDS RAISED FORE AND AFT AND ATTACHED BY STRAPS TO
THE SPRING HOOKS PROVIDED. NOTE THE MEN RUNNING TO THE
FRONT TO LIFT THE FORWARD HANDLES.

faces, very strong springs and ample wheelbase, so that the ambulance body shall not overhang the rear of the chassis to too great an extent. To form the complete vehicle, what is wanted at such times is not necessarily a luxuriously-equipped conveyance, but is rather a quite light and simple body sensibly constructed to bear its load, and capable of standing any amount of jolting without either its component parts shaking loose among themselves, or the body as a whole becoming insecure in its connections with the chassis.

As regards the interior equipments, in most instances all that is needed is provision for readily fixing in place two or four stretchers as the case may be, and also for loading the stretchers on to and unloading them off the body without difficulty, and without unnecessary discomfort to the patient. The standard types of ambulance body approved by the British Red Cross Society consist of simple but stout wooden frameworks with all the joints reinforced by angle irons held by bolts through the wooden members, and not merely by wood screws, which are liable to work loose. Over this framework is stretched a cover of waterproof canvas that has been treated with rubber, while the front and back of the vehicles are covered in by waterproof curtains of similar material, capable of being drawn aside or raised quite easily so as to enable attendants, with the minimum of difficulty, to lift the loaded stretchers into the vehicles.

Medical experts who have experience in the carriage of wounded men do not appear to be entirely in agreement as to whether the stretchers in a motor ambulance should be rigidly secured to the vehicle body, or should be carried by some form of springing supplementary to that of the car itself. In some examples of ambulances in regular use in this country, additional springing is provided by suspending the body from the chassis by means of semi-elliptical or complete elliptical springs. In many others, no springing other than that of the vehicle itself is interposed between the stretcher and the ground. One point at least on which there is universal agreement is that on no account must any rolling motion of the stretcher relative to the vehicle body be permitted, as motion of this kind causes acute discomfort to the patient, and often leads to physical effects similar to those occasioned by the rolling of a vessel at sea.

Probably side loading is the ideal method of getting stretchers on to an ambulance car, but it is difficult to realise the ideal in the case of a simple and fairly cheaply constructed body. Consequently, the system of end loading is far more common. In this case, the stretcher

A TOURING CAR EQUIPPED WITH A FOUR-STRETCHER AMBULANCE BODY BY MESSRS. BROWN, HUGHES AND STRACHAN, TO THE ORDER OF THE DUCHESS OF WESTMINSTER

is generally slipped in along the floor of the vehicle, and when right inside the car, is raised to the necessary elevation to allow it to be secured in position. The lower stretchers are afterwards slipped in and similarly secured. A design in which this is possible is more convenient than one in which the upper stretchers have to be raised to their full height before the operation of sliding them into the car can be attempted.

A type of fitting which has been adopted for some of the two-stretcher ambulances of the British Red Cross Society is that known as the L.X.R. It consists of a simple steel-tubed framework, the corner members of which are slotted to take the ball ends of cross bars from which the stretchers are slung by very short ropes and straps. When in position in the slots, the cross bar ends bear on the tops of strong spiral springs which relieve the stretcher of a certain amount of vibration, but at the same time, not being free to move other than in the vertical, do not set up any rolling motion. When these fittings, which are manufactured by Messrs. Simonis, are used, no weight is carried from any portion of the ambulance body except the floor. Consequently, the remainder of the construction can be very light and merely designed to support the waterproof covering. For four stretcher bodies the British Red Cross Society have at the time of writing been employing two main types.

In one of these, the stretchers merely slide in, the upper ones on to shelves and the lower ones along the floor, and are secured quite rigidly in position. In the other type, a system of spring suspension has been adopted. This latter system—evolved for the Society by Messrs. Brown, Hughes and Strachan—adapts itself to the construction of a simple, strong, but quite inexpensive body, to the main members of which are bolted iron arms which can be easily arranged so that they can be swung to one side while the car is being loaded, if it is considered that there is any risk of their interfering with the ease of the operation. Each of these iron arms has a flattened end, bored to take a vertical iron rod, the lower portion of which is formed into a hook, while the upper portion carries a heavy spiral spring concealed in a neat casing.

The stretchers are carried from the hooks by means of quite short leather straps, connecting the hooks with the stretcher handles. It will be noted that the springs allow of no movement other than one in a purely vertical direction, and consequently that practically no rolling should result from the use of this system, which has the advantage of giving an additional spring suspension at a very small increase in the cost of the complete body. A very considerable number of ambulances built on these lines have been supplied by the makers to the Red Cross Society.

It is impossible to lay too much emphasis on the desirability of using for ambulances, chassis with long wheelbase, in which the stretchers are as far as possible carried between the wheels, and the patients thereby protected from direct road shock. It is not to be expected that short wheel-based chassis carrying ambulance bodies with a big overhang at the rear, will prove durable over the broken roads of the countries in which war is taking place. If wheelbase is not sufficient to allow of the fitting of a four-stretcher body without these grave disadvantages, the only thing to do is to put up with the smaller accommodation of a two-stretcher body. The usual arrangement in this case is to extend the body right forward towards the dash on the left of the driver, and so to push the stretchers a couple of feet further forward, the space inside the body behind the driver serving for the carriage of luggage, for an attendant, or for one or two wounded men who are not very seriously injured.

One of the great dangers in this arrangement is that of obstructing the view of the driver towards his left. This is particularly serious when the car is for use in countries where the rule of the road is the reverse to our own, and where traffic in the opposite direction has to pass on the side upon which a free view is obscured. A possibility is to take in the space below the driver's seat and that alongside cf it, and to run in the patients on their stretchers, feet first, alongside of one another on the floor of the conveyance. In this way, about a foot of length can be economised, and with a two-stretcher body of this type it is of course not necessary for the super-structure to be either strong or high.

Another important point, if the cars are to go abroad and to be used under bad conditions of road surface, is that any ordinary simple method of attaching the body to the chassis must be very carefully examined before it is approved. Something more than average security is needed.

A fair number of touring cars are being changed into motor ambulances, not by replacement of the body but by its adaptation. This method has the disadvantage that it renders the old body subsequently useless for other purposes. Further, it is likely to cause delay, since every case has to be considered on its individual merits. Also, unless

A French Military Searchlight Motor. The searchlight is carried on an underframe, which can be let down in the manner shown. The electricity is supplied from the motive power of the car.

the chassis is a long one, the adaptation will almost certainly involve a big overhang.

These notes will serve to give the necessary information to those who may wish to equip motor ambulances for any kind of use during the war, and there does not appear to be any need to go into details of all the various other varieties of ambulance body, many of them very beautifully fitted and designed, but also very expensive. One other type may, however, be mentioned, since it is being employed extensively by the French and Belgian Governments. This consists essentially of a stout floor carrying two iron frameworks of inverted V shape. Between these two and stretching fore and aft is an arrangement similar in principle to a squirrel cage, or to a water-wheel with four floats.

The place of each float is taken by the necessary apparatus for the support of a stretcher, provision being made that all the four stretchers retain their horizontal position whatever the position of the framework supporting them. The stretchers can be loaded in from the side to the bottom position, and the apparatus swung round so that this operation is continued, the stretchers after being loaded being subsequently raised by the rotation of the frame. It is stated that in Antwerp and elsewhere this type of ambulance has been used extensively, and is found to be very comfortable and very easy to construct.

Turning to the work for which the ambulances are being employed, much of this is of an obvious character. Ambulance services are evidently needed both at the military hospitals, and also further back at the big base hospitals of the Red Cross Society on the Continent. They are wanted again at all the various hospitals in this country to which wounded men are brought. They are employed, for example, in London, to meet the hospital trains and carry from the stations those men who are not able to be conveyed in ordinary cars.

The requirement of motor ambulances nearer the front is almost limitless. In the system of the R.A.M.C. in service, wounded men are first removed by regimental stretcher-bearers to the "aid post," where medical attention is first given to them. Thence, they are carried by the bearer sections of the field ambulance—and possibly, if roads permit, by motor ambulances—to the advance dressing stations, whence after treatment they are taken by the military ambulance waggons to meet conveyances from the clearing hospital, which is usually situated somewhere near the railhead. Upon this hospital falls the duty of avoiding all overcrowding nearer the front, and this must be done by

AN OPEN TOURING CAR CONVERTED INTO A MOTOR AMBULANCE

employing all available means of transport.

Evidently, motor ambulances are the most suitable kind of conveyance for this work, since they afford a reasonable degree of comfort to the patient, and even if their speed capacities cannot be utilised to any great extent while they are carrying wounded men, advantage can be taken of them while returning empty towards the front for further load. Once the patients have been taken as far back; as the field hospital at railhead, their subsequent conveyance to the Red Cross hospitals, or any other required points, can be carried out by train supplemented by local motor ambulance services from; the termini to the hospitals.

Another and less obvious type of service is that which involves thorough patrolling of all those districts in which battles have taken place, with a view to ascertaining whether any wounded men are still remaining in the villages and along the countryside, where they may be given thoroughly kind, but possibly somewhat unskilled, attention by the civilian inhabitants. Another duty of the drivers of the ambulances carrying out this work is that of setting on foot minute inquiries with a view to finding out whether any men killed in battle have been buried by civilians without any record having become available which would serve as a basis for certain information which can never be so terrible as an almost hopeless state of suspense.

This class of work, of course, has to be carried out over roads which have in many cases been badly broken up by heavy military traffic, and possibly even intentionally destroyed by a retreating enemy. Consequently, it puts a very severe strain on every portion of the chassis and body of the ambulance, and makes the fact that the whole of the motor vehicles at present employed by the Society have been freely given or lent by their owners without reservation and without charge all the more noteworthy.

For some time past, the Society has been shipping ambulance cars, and also touring cars, to the Continent as rapidly as means of transit have permitted. The requirement seems to be enormous, but even so there does not appear to be any likelihood of the supply falling short of it. Many motorists have placed not only their cars, but their own services ungrudgingly at the disposal of the Society. The usual practice is for the Society, after accepting a car for service, to undertake to have a suitable ambulance body put upon it in place of its own. In some cases, however, motorists have even taken this charge upon themselves, and whatever may be the disadvantages of dependence upon volunteer service, it can at least be said that in this case such dependence

A TYPE OF EXTEMPORISED MOTOR AMBULANCE FAVOURED BY THE FRENCH AND BELGIANS

has served in some measure to show how many men, unable for one reason or another to take up military duties, are only too anxious to expend their energies and their money on any object of national value in connection with which they are able to be of use.

CHAPTER 6

The Transport of Ammunition and Artillery

The system of maintaining ammunition supplies for troops in the field is very similar to that already described in connection with the supply of food. Stocks of ammunition are kept at depots of the Army Ordnance Corps at various points between the base and railhead, to which they are forwarded as required. From railhead they are brought forward daily by the motor lorries of the divisional ammunition parks to a convenient refilling point, where they are transhipped on to horsed ammunition carts for distribution in detail. With the troops entirely dependent on the motor vehicle for the maintenance of their supplies both of food and of ammunition, there is no need to labour the enormous importance of mechanical transport in modern warfare, or the terrible consequences which would follow anything approaching a general failure in the reliability of the machines used.

For the haulage of very heavy guns some form of engine power is of course essential, and the ordinary steam traction engine provides the most obvious solution, since it is to be assumed that if the roads and bridges to be traversed are sufficiently strong to bear the gun itself, they will also bear the engines which haul it. The big traction engine is a very British product, and it is interesting, if not quite satisfactory, to note that the huge siege guns of the German Army are stated to be hauled by engines of British origin. For lighter guns, the steam tractor, or small traction engine, can be employed, but very many efforts have been made to dispense with its service in favour of an internal combustion tractor, less dependent on constant renewal of fuel and water supplies.

In the brief sketch already given of the principal trials and ma-

A British "Marshall" internal combustion tractor suitable for the haulage of artillery

noeuvres in which motor transport has figured, some indication has been afforded of the attempts made by the British Government in this direction. The most consistent, and probably the most successful, efforts have however been made by our neighbours, the French, who have for this special purpose given much encouragement to the development of internal combustion tractors driving all four wheels. The movement dates back about three years, and owes its origin to the need for hauling 155 m/m siege guns along roads and across country. The first type of tractor produced to meet the requirement was the Chatillon-Panhard. The weight of the first type with full load was in the neighbourhood of 22 tons, and more recently efforts have been made to evolve lighter types weighing about 14 tons with their load, the belief being that these rather smaller machines would be of great general utility.

Some very important trials in this connection took place in France early in 1914, four types of tractor participating, namely, the Latil, the Schneider, the Chatillon-Panhard and the Renault. The first-named is a development of the Latil type of lorry, in which the engines drive the front wheels, and the whole power plant is concentrated on to the fore carriage, the back wheels and the platform being really nothing more in principle than a two-wheeled trailing vehicle. An extension of this system involves the use of three differential gears, one for each pair of wheels, and a third as a balance gear half way along the vehicle from which the drive is taken fore and aft through longitudinal shafts and worm gearing. All four wheels are steered as well as driven.

In the Schneider, the drive is taken from a gear box containing two sets of sliding gears through cardan shafts to the front and back axles, and alternatively, when required, to a capstan enabling the engine to haul through the medium of a wire rope. In the Chatillon-Panhard, the transmission is so arranged as to involve no universal joints, and only one differential gear. This is mounted on a transverse counter-shaft, and the power is taken to the wheels through bevel gears at the ends of the countershaft, and four diagonal shafts driving in their turn auxiliary shafts upon which are bevels engaging with similar bevels on the wheels. The Renault is a very simple machine of its type. The drive is taken fore and aft from the gear box by cardan shafts leading to differential gears on the front and back axle.

Either one of the differentials can be locked when desired to help the machine to find its way out of difficult positions. Yet another machine which is available to the French Government, though it did

A French petrol-electric four-wheel-drive tractor, the wheels of which are specially shod to facilitate travelling over rough ground.

not take part in the trials mentioned, employs electrical machinery in place of the usual mechanical transmission gear. The engine drives an electric dynamo, which supplies current to four electric motors, one for each wheel. On the whole, the French four-wheel driven tractors have performed very well under severe tests, and it is stated that approximately 300 tractors of one or other of the types mentioned are available for military service, though it is possible that this estimate is somewhat exaggerated.

For the rapid transport of light artillery various special machines have been devised, providing either for the carriage of a gun upon the platform of a motor lorry, or for the construction of a gun-carrying vehicle forming one complete unit. In this branch of development the Germans have shown the most initiative, and Krupps have got out several interesting designs. In all of these strong motor lorry chassis are used. A usual system is to fit, by hinging to the back of the chassis, strong ramps up which the gun may be hauled, either by the power of the motor engine or by other means. When on the platform, the gun wheels sink into depressions formed to take them and also bear up against shaped vertical stops. When the gun is in place the ramps are swung over, and are so designed that their ends can then be conveniently attached rigidly to the vertical stops, the ramps themselves also bearing against the gun wheels and holding them quite secure; or in an alternative method, the ramps are arranged to grip the axle of the gun-carriage.

Special designs are for motor vehicles capable of a good turn of speed, and arranged to carry guns especially intended for fighting against aeroplanes or airships, and consequently so arranged as to allow of their muzzles being swung up until the gun assumes a vertical position.

Other special arrangements of motor vehicles are those providing for the carriage of machine guns, but this type perhaps comes more properly under the title of an armoured motor car.

A KRUPP GUN-CARRYING LORRY, SHOWING THE RAMPS UP WHICH THE GUN HAS BEEN HAULED SERVING ALSO THE PURPOSE OF HOLDING IT SECURELY IN POSITION.

CHAPTER 7

Armoured Cars and Other Military Motors

While everyone was aware that the heavy motor would play a very important part in the great war in connection with the transport of supplies and artillery, and that touring cars would be largely used for staff purposes, the enormous extent to which the armoured car has been employed has probably come as something of a surprise. We were, of course, aware of the existence of such machines, but up to the present there had been no real proof of their utility. The German military authorities had evidently, prior to the war, come to their own conclusions on the matter, and the Belgians, whether they were prepared in advance or not, were at least very prompt in following suit.

It is doubtful whether, when the war broke out, our own War Department was in possession of a single armoured car, but fortunately this is a type of machine in connection with which deficiencies can be very rapidly made up, and at the time of writing, while no certain quantitative information is available, we are at least aware of the existence of British armoured cars on the Continent, and we know that, for example, London motor omnibuses have been equipped for this class of duty. In this, and in most cases, the improvised armoured car is merely an ordinary vehicle with some simple form of body covered over by armour plating, and with the more vital portions of its mechanism to some degree similarly protected.

Thus, some protection is provided for the radiator and steering gear. The dash is covered by steel plating extending upwards to protect the driver, while the platform or body behind is protected by vertical or sloping steel plates. Certain examples of German armoured cars that have been captured answer sufficiently well to this description, but

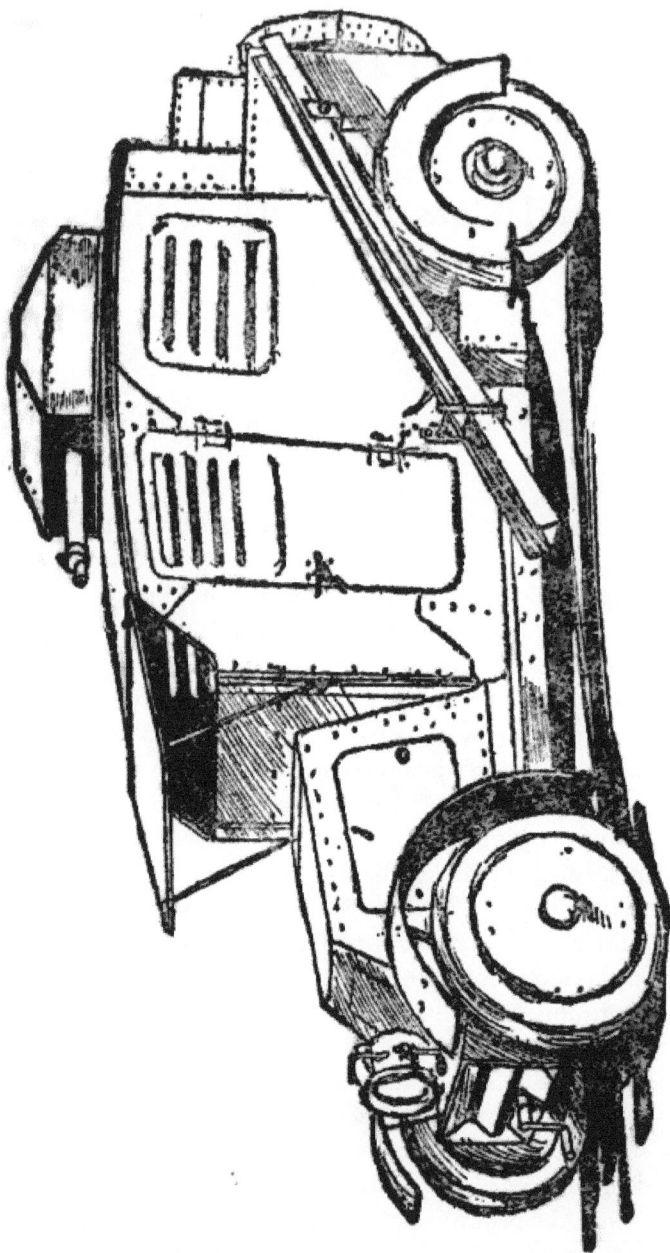

A "Charron" armoured car with machine gun.

naturally enough in a country where the supply of industrial vehicles is more or less inadequate, the touring car has been selected for adaptation. It has, of course, the advantage of extra speed, and the disadvantage of the vulnerability of pneumatic tyres. Some of these improvised armoured cars merely carry men armed with rifles, while others are equipped with light machine guns. In many instances, searchlights, or very strong head lamps, are fitted. The latter can, of course, be operated by the now familiar electric system, a small dynamo and a battery of cells being carried upon the car.

The most convenient arrangement for a more powerful searchlight is to be found in the use of a petrol-electric vehicle in which the ordinary change-speed gears are dispensed with, and their place taken by electric machines. The car engine drives a dynamo which generates electric current. This is supplied to an electric motor from which the power is transmitted to the rear wheels. The arrangement is tantamount to an infinitely variable change speed gear, and the important point in connection with the subject under consideration is that the whole or part of the engine power can be used for generating electric current, which can be easily applied to a searchlight on the car.

Armoured cars carrying powerful lights are no doubt very effective for reconnoitring during the night. The lights can be switched on quite suddenly and some damage inflicted upon an enemy, and the light switched off again before there is time for fire to be returned or the machine to be located effectively. The car can then be moved rapidly to some other point, and the manoeuvre repeated. In general, the armoured car has been used as a kind of advance guard in front of the screen of cavalry which performs the double duty of concealing the movement of its own infantry and locating the forces of the enemy. Just as the Germans employed cavalry for this purpose to an unprecedented extent in the Franco-Prussian war of 1870, and so gained an enormous advantage over their opponents, so the attempt has been made on this occasion to utilise a still more rapid and effective means towards the same ends.

As already suggested, any advantage that may have accrued from the utilisation of a new method of this kind need only be a purely temporary one, since any desired quantity of the enormous number of available machines can—if it appears desirable—be converted into armoured cars for our own use or that of our allies at very short notice. One would imagine that events will prove that the armoured motor is valuable as an irritant rather than as a means of locating

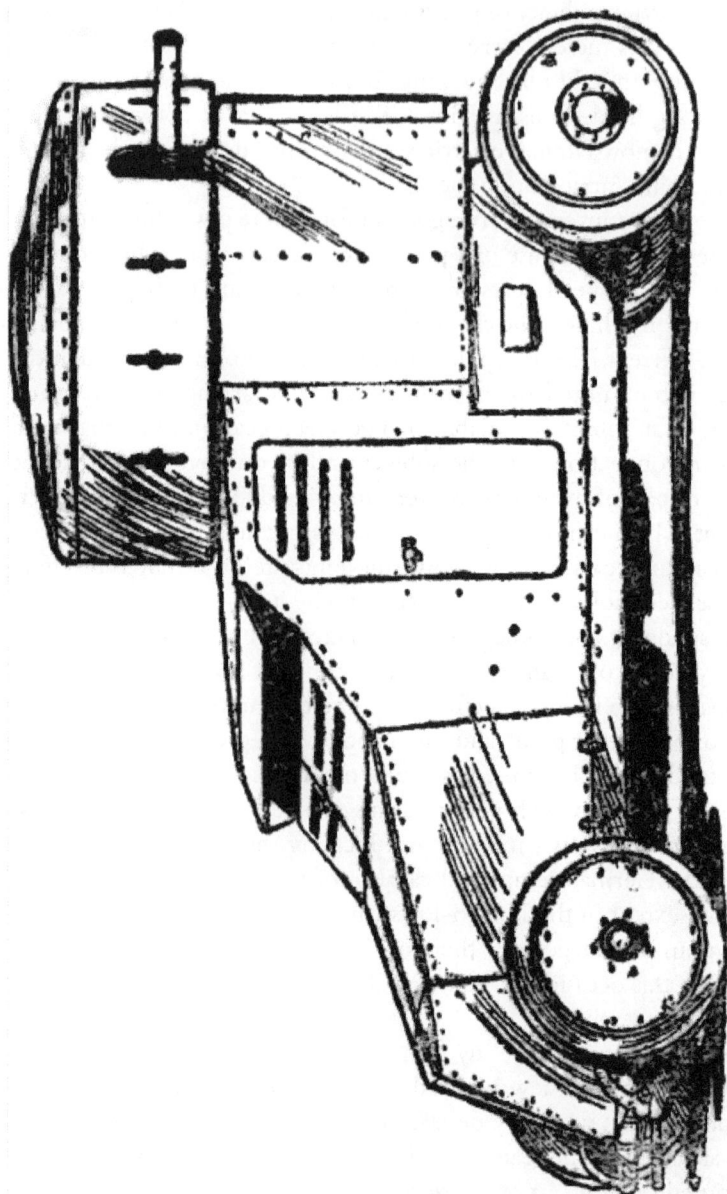

A "SCHNEIDER" ARMOURED CAR WITH QUICK-FIRING GUN.

hostile forces or screening one's own, since both these latter ends are very much affected by the use of aeroplanes, which make it practically impossible to move large bodies of men secure from observation, and correspondingly easy to gather fairly accurate information as to the whereabouts and strength of the enemy.

So far we have touched only upon extemporised armoured vehicles as distinct from those actually designed in the first instance for this specific duty. The first armoured car was produced as long ago as 1896. The design was published in *The Autocar* only a week after the Act which permitted a motorcar to exceed four miles an hour on British roads, and to dispense with the man walking in front with a red flag, came into force. The suggestion emanated from the late Mr. E. J. Pennington, and the machine, the mechanism of which was necessarily somewhat primitive, was arranged to carry two small machine guns the cranks of which were to be driven by the car engine with a view to increasing the rapidity of fire.

In those days, the machine gun was usually hand-cranked. At intervals since that time various designs had been brought out, the general principle being to employ a completely armoured car, the driver of which would in most cases be in considerable danger of accident, owing to the way in which the protection provided for him obscured the view of the road on either side. In the majority of cases, the vehicle was designed to carry one machine gun mounted in a turret above the roof. Thus, in a design got out by the Charron Company some time back, the machine gun was contained in a rotating turret a little way forward of the rear axle. The joint between this turret and the roof of the car involved a flange and a thick rubber ring. The turret rotated on a central vertical shaft, and on this shaft was a screw wheel.

The effect of turning this wheel was to raise or lower the turret. When the machine gun had been drawn into the right position with the turret raised, the wheel was turned bringing the turret down hard against the rubber ring which held it securely, and prevented it from shaking about while the gun was being fired.

In another design, coming from the Creusot Works of Messrs. Schneider, provision was made for a larger machine gun, carried in a substantial turret projecting from the car roof, and mounted upon rollers running on an inwardly projecting ring on the lower fixed portion of the turret. This ring was toothed on its inner side and engaged with a gear wheel enabling the turret, and with it the gun, to be swung round into the desired position. The gun itself carried a seat, and the

An Italian design for a motor battery of quick-firing guns. The sides swivel round to face in any desired position.

gear for rotating the turret was connected with pedals, so that a man sitting on the gun could rotate it and the turret by the action of his feet, keeping his hands free for the refinements of aiming and working the weapon.

Reference may be made to one more design for which an Italian officer was responsible. In this case, the vehicle formed a kind of moving battery of machine guns, mounted so as normally to point out of the sides of the car. Each half of the body, however, was capable of being swung round on hinges either at the back or at the front, and castors were provided to facilitate its motion. Thus, when the car was stationary, it was possible to swing round the whole of its armament so as to face the front, rear, or either side.

If the general conclusion as to the utility of armoured motor cars bears out the impressions formed in the earlier portions of the war, there can be little doubt that these more comprehensive designs will receive in the near future consideration which has been denied to them in the past, and that types of armoured car will be evolved as much more effective than the extemporised patterns as our armoured cruisers are when compared with converted merchant ships.

Without devoting too much space to the consideration of machines which are as yet merely proposals and not actualities, brief mention may be made of a design recently got out by a British engineer, and representing in a sense the last word in armoured cars, since it is in no sense a make-shift, and provides for the complete protection of the driver and every item of the mechanism. The car is, of course, completely enclosed, and from its roof projects an armoured turret containing two machine guns. The driver gets his view of the road only through louvres in front and in the side doors.

The lines of the car consist of a series of curves which are preferred to flat surfaces, in order to increase to a maximum the possibility of deflecting any bullets which strike the vehicle. Even the radiator and the tyres are armoured. The former is situated against the dashboard, and has above it a cover in the shape of a cupola through which the air is drawn down by a fan round the vertical tubes. Each wheel is built up of two steel discs, one inside the other, and an air tube covered by strong fabric is placed between the two. The outer disc is allowed sufficient freedom of movement to enable the arrangement to approximate the pneumatic tyre in effect, while being completely protected from puncture from any cause.

It is reasonable to suppose that the near future will see considerable

A "Minerva" armoured car with machine gun

developments in the armoured motorcar in two directions, namely, in the direction of the vehicle designed and constructed throughout for a specific purpose, and also in the direction of the lightly armoured fast touring car available for staff and scouting purposes.

This last brings us to the subject of a very valuable sphere of activity of motors in warfare. There is, however, but little to be written on this point, since the general use of cars by staff officers from the commander-in-chief downwards may be taken for granted, and the employment of fast vehicles for scouting purposes and by officers of the Intelligence Department is equally self-evident. For the carrying of dispatches and other such work, the motorcycle is being found extremely useful. This, the lightest class of motor vehicle, is also used in conjunction with its heavier relations. Motorcyclists, who are usually skilled mechanics, are attached to all the heavy motor transport columns, their duties being to scout ahead, to keep the units of the column together, and also to assist in the event of any roadside trouble.

Motors of all kinds are extensively used in connection with the flying corps. To each squadron of aeroplanes a number of motors are attached for various duties. Some may act as first-aid machines, and for the carriage of spare parts. Other larger and heavier motors are employed for the carriage of partially dismantled aeroplanes. Others, again, are fitted up as workshops to help in the important work of repairing and keeping in tune the engines and mechanisms of the aeroplanes. As regards other important uses of motors in warfare, brief mention should at least be made of the cars fitted with wireless telegraphy equipments, and portable searchlights, and also of motor field kitchens.

CHAPTER 8

The Provision of Military Motor Transport

Having decided definitely that a complete system of motor transport must be employed primarily in order to secure greater efficiency and freedom of movement of troops in the field, the next step is to decide upon the best means of securing the availability of the necessary number of suitable vehicles m time of war. Evidently, the simplest procedure would be to depend solely and entirely upon the power of the government to commandeer or requisition the required supplies. At first sight it may appear that nothing more is needed, but any such conclusion would be highly erroneous. If we were to examine the fleet of any large motor omnibus, motor cab, or motor haulage concern, we should almost inevitably find that the vehicles employed were almost all of one make and commonly of one type.

If an operating company has in the first instance decided to adopt a particular make of vehicle, and if subsequent improvement in design reduces the efficiency of the original type as compared with others of the market, then the natural move is not to change from one manufacturer to another, but to increase or partially renew the fleet by the purchase of new vehicles of the same make but of a more modern model. The change from the old to the new type does not involve alterations in by any means every part of the mechanism, but only in those parts which have in any way shown themselves capable of improvement. In the event of renewals being required, it is not then necessary to stock an entirely new set of spare parts for all portions of the car, but only to get in spares for those parts, the design of which has been changed and improved.

In this way, the necessary stock of spare parts is so far as possible reduced, and the work of maintaining the cars is in a similar degree simplified. Almost every type of motor vehicle has its own peculiarities, and it is evidently easier for a mechanic to undertake the maintenance of a certain number of machines all of one make than to keep in running order a similar number of miscellaneous vehicles varying essentially from one another.

Then again, the standardisation of one make is an advantage, because for purposes of maintenance the number of workshop appliances required is reduced to a minimum, and it is possible in some cases to obtain machines specially adapted for turning out in quantity some particular part which figures largely in the maintenance of the fleet.

Yet another advantage is that the driver of any one car can, without danger or loss of efficiency, be put on to any other car, if his own is undergoing repair or overhaul, while the work of those departments concerned with the storing and issuing of parts is greatly simplified, and the accommodation required for the efficient operation of the whole concern is reduced.

If these arguments apply to an industrial organisation working under normal conditions, they apply still more strongly to a hastily enlarged temporary organisation evolved in time of war. Moreover, in the latter case the unreliable running of a fleet of cars does not represent merely a temporary financial loss or a diminution in prestige. Its result must inevitably be to cause, among the troops behind which the motor column is working, a lack of necessities either in respect of food or of warlike materials. In either case, the result is immeasurable and the consequences may well prove fatal.

Then again, military motor vehicles are required to work under peculiarly arduous and trying conditions. The very nature of their service implies frequent long runs under the worst possible conditions of weather and road surface. They may have to employ lanes or bye-ways or even routes which can hardly be described as roads at all, and added to this is the almost certain fact that the tracks over which they work will have been materially injured intentionally or otherwise.

Those who live in the vicinity of any important military centre must be well aware of the damaging effect that heavy military traffic has upon the roads, even if well-constructed, in view of the inevitable nature of the traffic. When plying on country roads never intended for such use, the transport motors themselves will soon break up the road surface. These considerations serve to show that the liability to breakdown is much greater in military than in civilian transport, and coupled with this is the certainty that the facilities for conveniently carrying out repairs and overhauls must necessarily be extremely limited. The transport columns are supported at their base by travelling workshops manned by skilled mechanics and containing small selections of those tools likely to be of the most general service. The equipment of these workshops must be reduced to a minimum in order to secure their portability, and it is highly important, if possible, to prevent jobs coming in which cannot be satisfactorily tackled with the machinery at the disposal of the mechanical staff.

It will thus be seen that everything points to the extreme inadvisability of depending upon motor transport and supply columns formed of a miscellaneous collection of vehicles of all types, all makes and all ages. Looking at the other side of the question, the ideal conditions are reached when every vehicle of the column is identical and represents the very best make and type, and when all the drivers are thoroughly acquainted with the idiosyncrasies of this particular type of vehicle, and the mechanics responsible for repairs equally experienced as regards every feature of the mechanism of the machines.

To secure something approaching true standardisation in a fleet of transport vehicles, either one or two alternative methods may be adopted. The first and most obvious is that of direct purchase by government. At the moment of writing, this system is being extensively adopted in Great Britain, and doubtless also in all other belligerent countries in which it has been possible to keep suitable motor manufacturing works in operation. Such steps are, however, being taken, in order to meet a great emergency which has arisen before alternative schemes have had time fully to mature.

The establishment of an army in time of peace is very much less than it is in war time, and in time of war an army must be far more self-supporting than it is in time of peace, when considerable quantities of supplies can be brought regularly by civilian contractors to depots where the troops are stationed, and the military authorities require only to secure the distribution of such supplies in detail. In time of war the whole of the supplies must be delivered in bulk to a very limited number of points, and from that time onwards the military authorities must be responsible for what may be described as their wholesale as well as their retail distribution.

Added to this are a number of other considerations, as, for example, the fact that when on active service the scale of rations of the men is increased, and supplies of warlike stores are rapidly expended and have

A French motor workshop, especially equipped for the
service of the Flying Corps.

A German workshop car, closed to take the road

to be perpetually renewed. It is clear, then, that if the method of direct purchase alone is depended upon, either the supply of motor vehicles will be immensely greater than the useful requirement hi times of peace, or else facilities must be created for increasing their supply instantaneously when mobilisation occurs, or the organisation of new armies becomes essential.

Now, as in the present instance, it is possible after a war has begun to provide for a steady and considerable supply of transport motors to be handed over to the military authorities week by week, provided always that the process of manufacturing is not seriously interfered with either by the propinquity of military operations, or by the need of drafting men in excessive numbers from the works to the active forces. In our own case, it is quite within the bounds of possibility to produce motors for the transport columns of new armies just as rapidly as it is possible to make the personnel of those new armies effective. This fact, however, does not cover the difficulty occasioned by the necessary increase in transport facilities for the standing army directly war breaks out. It has been suggested that the difficulty might be overcome if the War Department were to purchase large numbers of suitable motor lorries, and to employ the greater part of them in time of peace for the carriage of general goods.

This scheme has the advantage that it not only provides the necessary fleet, but simultaneously trains the necessary drivers; nevertheless, it has the grave drawback that profitable employment of the kind required could not be found unless the government were to enter into serious competition with haulage and delivery companies. It has been proposed also that numbers of suitable motors might be used normally in the service of the Post Office, and transferred on emergency to the War Department, but this again is open to objection. The Post Office fleets would have to be renewed hurriedly and under difficulties, and a certain amount of disorganisation would almost certainly result. Furthermore, the number of vehicles which could be usefully kept in service by the postal authorities is small compared with the increased military requirements occasioned by the outbreak of war.

We may take it, then, that the principle of maintaining in the possession of the War Department in time of peace sufficient motor vehicles to fill the whole of the needs in time of war is unworkable except at enormous cost, since the majority of the vehicles could be put to no useful work and would merely deteriorate and become obsolete and, therefore, comparatively speaking, valueless were they to stand

TWO VIEWS OF PARTS OF THE BRITISH "KARRIER"
SUBVENTION TYPE LORRY, INDICATING THE EFFORTS MADE TO
FACILITATE INSPECTION AND REPLACEMENTS.
THE ENGINE VALVES WITH INSPECTION COVER REMOVED.

HOW THE AXLE SHAFTS CAN BE WITHDRAWN. BY REMOVING THE
TOP AND BOTTOM CASING, THE WHOLE OF THE FINAL GEARING,
INCLUDING THE DIFFERENTIAL, CAN BE REMOVED WITHOUT
JACKING UP THE VEHICLE OR TAKING OFF THE LOAD.

idle. The whole of such a fleet would have to be replaced every three or four years, and if this were not done an enemy equipped with more modern vehicles would possess a marked advantage, since—though the motor industry has now assumed enormous proportions—it is still so young that progress in design is by no means stationary.

We now come to the question of whether it is possible to maintain in time of peace only the number of vehicles actually required, and to fill up the requirement in excess of this number as promptly as possible, but nevertheless with some delay, when war breaks out. On this point, Captain A. E. Davidson, R.E., a former Secretary of the Mechanical Transport Committee of the War Office, has given the following very definite opinion in a paper read by him at the Imperial Motor Transport Conference, in his official capacity as representative of the War Department:

> Emphasis must be laid on the necessity for obtaining the transport immediately. The army which can mobilise in the shortest space of time gains an immense advantage by being able to take the initiative before the opposing armies are prepared, and the army which mobilises most rapidly will be able to gain a decisive advantage. This question has now been so carefully worked out in detail that the complete mobilisation of an army can be arranged for within a period that is reckoned in hours.

To meet this requirement, the additional motor transport columns must also be capable of being mobilised with similar rapidity, and we are forced back either on to the last resort of commandeering any vehicle that comes handy, or else on to the preparation of a scheme which will provide a substantial reserve of vehicles of approved make and type, able to be made available at any instant at a few hours' notice. Such a scheme evidently involves the payment to the owners of these vehicles of some sum intended to make up to them such loss as may result from their liability to have their vehicles immediately commandeered. These payments, moreover, must provide that the War Department shall have the right of periodical inspection of the cars, so that they may be well informed as to their condition, and may have certain knowledge as to whether they are being properly driven and maintained in such a way as to make them useful units of a fleet on active service.

A scheme of this sort is called a "subvention" or "subsidy" scheme, and it is very generally admitted that such a scheme forms an essential part of the organisation of transport and supply in every country in which the civilian use of heavy motor vehicles is sufficiently extensive to make the principle of subsidy applicable on a working scale. Clearly, the amount of the subsidy which is offered to owners of motor vehicles of a suitable type must depend, in the first instance, on the conditions accompanying the payments. If—as to some extent in the case of Great Britain—the subsidy scheme applies only to vehicles of types which would not be employed for trade purposes were definite encouragement not offered by the government, the payments must be more than sufficient to balance any disadvantages resulting from the use of the subsidy type vehicle, as well as the inconvenience of undergoing inspections.

Again, if the War Department makes various stipulations as to features to be embodied in the design of subsidy vehicles, it is more or less certain that these stipulations will entail manufacturing expenditure resulting in an increase in the sale price of the machines as compared with the price of ordinary models of similar carrying capacity. Thus, the subsidy must also be sufficient to cover any increase in first cost to the user. If this increase is, let us say, £50, and the inconveniences entailed by adopting the type result in a loss of efficiency estimated, let us say, at £30 a year, the subsidy, if it is to form any real inducement, must evidently amount to a payment on purchase of about £60 at the least, followed by a payment of, let us say, £40 a year for three or four years.

In countries where heavy motor vehicles are not—unless some abnormal encouragement is given—sufficiently extensively used for trade purposes, the subsidy must of course be considerably higher. If the conditions of service are so unfavourable to the use of mechanical transport as to convince the trader that in changing, let us say, from twenty horses and five waggons to a couple of 3-ton motor lorries, his expenses will be increased by £100 or £200 a year, the scheme must take this prospective loss into account. In that case, the scheme becomes something more than mere subsidy, and partakes more of the nature of a scheme designed artificially to en courage the use of a particular form of transport solely on account of its utility to the government in case of war.

CHAPTER 9

A Comparison of National
Conditions

In considering how far any form of subsidy scheme has been, or
could be, truly successful, we have to take into account first of all the
national and local conditions governing the use of motor vehicles in
ordinary commercial service, and it is satisfactory to be able to record
that a consideration of this subject leads to the conclusion that the
position of Great Britain is peculiarly advantageous, inasmuch as the
number of industrial motor vehicles in service is vastly in excess of
the total requirement of the British Army, a state of affairs a parallel to
which does not exist in any other European country.

The economical use of motors in trade and industry depends in
the first case very largely upon the quality and quantity of the national roads. Great Britain is fortunate in the possession of the finest
road system in the world. We are not limited as regards motor haulage
by the absence of thoroughfares between our industrial or residential
districts, and it is possible to deliver goods to practically every house
or even cottage in the kingdom, without having to traverse anything
worse than a short distance of rather rough country lane or private
track.

There is no doubt that London has been very largely responsible
for the enormous development of motor transport within the British
Isles. It is generally considered that Paris represents the nearest approach to London for purposes of comparison. Nevertheless, the population of Paris is only about half that of London, and the area within
which that population is included is only about one quarter. In other
words, the density of population of Paris is double that of London,
which means that the average distance to be traversed in delivering

goods to a given number of people is much smaller in Paris than it is here. Now the motor vehicle is able to show superior economy over horse-drawn traffic mainly where it is able to make use of its capacity for speed and its ability to cover, without tiring, long distances in the course of a day. For house-to-house deliveries the motor is at a disadvantage, since while it is standing waiting before a door it represents a larger idle capital than the horsed cart, and the investment of this larger capital can only be justified if it results in the vehicle performing in a given time a far larger amount of work than would be possible if horses were used.

Taking, for example, the case of a 2-ton motor van capable of running about 100 miles in the course of a working day, the ideal condition is represented by a run under full load from the warehouse or store to some point about 50 miles distant. Here the whole load is delivered, and a complete return load is found. Such conditions are seldom available in practice, but the nearer it is possible to approach to them, the more likely is the motor to prove a profitable investment. On the other hand, supposing the car to be used for house-to-house work involving, let us say, 100 deliveries in the course of a day with a total distance covered of only about 10 miles, the motor may cover this distance in traffic in something like an hour, whereas a horsed vehicle might take two hours. The saving in that case is comparatively small, and represents, let us say, only an additional 10 deliveries or an advantage of 10 *per cent*, extra in the work done in the day. On the other hand, the cost of the motor is very much higher, and it is more than likely that on economical grounds the operating concern would not be justified in adopting mechanical transport.

Applying these examples of extreme cases to the general proposition, it is quite evident that both the larger population and the more scattered distribution of population of London make the metropolis a far more favourable nursery for the industrial motor than, let us say, Paris, or, for that matter, Berlin or Vienna. The great London houses have found that their conditions of delivery into outlying residential districts have been on the whole very favourable to motor transport, which they have consequently adopted extensively, favouring as a rule vans carrying loads varying between 25 cwt. and 3 or 4 tons, according to the nature of the goods to be handled.

By establishing motor services they have been able in many instances to dispense with local distributing depots in the environs of London, and they have found it possible greatly to extend their areas of direct delivery. One of the consequences has been that people resident 20, 30 or even 40 miles out of town are now able to place orders at big London houses, and to have the goods delivered direct to their own doors the same day, or at the latest on the following day. This delivery is effected without any unnecessary handling, and without any of that delay which must result if the railway is used as an intermediary.

By thus extending their field of operations, the big London houses have come directly into competition with the larger trading concerns centred in towns some distance from London. These local concerns have found that they were losing business to the London houses, and have been compelled in the interests of self-preservation to endeavour to retain that business by offering equally good and prompt facilities for delivery. Even so, some portion of their trade is necessarily lost to them, and they are compelled to seek new fields. In order to do this and to resist competition so far as may be, they are practically forced to adopt motor transport, and in their turn to extend their area until it embraces other towns and villages at a greater distance from the metropolis.

Thus, the influence of London steadily spreads outwards encouraging the adoption of motor transport in other towns. A similar phenomenon takes place in a smaller degree round all of our very numerous big industrial cities, with the result that the motor van and the motor lorry have become familiar objects in every part of the country, and have, so to speak, acted as a moving advertisement of their own utility.

This process, coupled with the comparative excellence of our roads, has favoured the general adoption of motor haulage by traders of all classes throughout the country. The railways have in consequence felt the effects of the competition of the motor vehicle, and have retaliated by putting themselves into possession of considerable fleets, in order to secure the rapid distribution of the goods entrusted to them for delivery. In some instances, railway companies have established services in country districts to act as feeders to their branch or main lines. Simultaneously, the general development, initiated in the first case by private enterprise, has become so marked and has proved so conclusively the reliability of the heavy motor, that Government Departments—notably the General Post Office—have been impressed with the great possibilities of the new transport, and have adopted motor vans for long distance services as well as for local distribution of mails in great cities, as being more direct as well as more economical than the old arrangements with the railways. This applies particularly to the carriage of parcels.

Side by side with this development has come the astonishing progress of the passenger motor vehicle. Here again, London has been the big moving influence. The greatest city in the world has grown from small beginnings according to its own sweet will. It has not been laid out, as have younger towns, with any clear scheme in view for meeting the growth of traffic requirements. Here again, the nearest parallel is to be found in Paris. Portions of that city are still similar to, or even worse than, London in this respect, and are traversed only by narrow and winding roads laid out on no intelligible scheme. Paris, however, has the advantage that for the past one hundred years definite methods of improvement have been pushed. Control has remained vested in the same departments, and the policy has been continuous. Consequently, the network of small streets has gradually become subordinate to an admirable system of main thoroughfares of great width and beauty, at the intersections of which are wide open places generally utilised for the erection of some of those fine monuments so dear to the French nation.

Other and newer towns, of which Berlin may be taken as a fine typical example, have been from the first almost wholly constructed in accordance with a definite town planning scheme, and in all their later developments the tramcar has been regarded as a necessity of passenger transport, and every provision has been made to ensure that a complete system of railed traffic should be in every way facilitated, and so far as possible prevented from injuring the natural and architectural beauties, which must at all cost be maintained in the interests of trade prosperity as well as from aesthetic reasons.

In such cases, the motor omnibus has from the start come into direct competition with the electric tramcar, the latter being generally supported by enormously influential vested interests, the strength of which has been such as to cripple, or almost entirely prevent, the introduction of public service motors. Both in Paris and in London, conditions for one reason or another have opposed the universal adoption of railed transport in the streets. So far as London is concerned, the tramcar is useful and possible in suburban districts, and as a means of bringing people to within a short distance of the central areas.

Beyond that point, its extension is probably impracticable, and is certainly open to very grave opposition, which has up to the present prevented the completion of anything approaching a comprehensive tramway system from north to south or from east to west. The central area a few years ago was served by the horsed omnibus, and it was with this vehicle and not with the tramcar that the motor omnibus in its early stages had to compete. Consequently, it was given a good opportunity of proving its desirable qualities and was not hopelessly handicapped by being set, when in very early and imperfect stages of development, directly against a more or less perfected system of passenger transport on rails. London has thus proved to be the world's biggest nursery of the motor omnibus. Its early imperfections caused plenty of grumbling and a certain amount of inconvenience, but it was realised all along that it was only a matter of time before it would oust the horse omnibus from the streets.

In Paris also, the motor omnibus has been given fair chances, and has proved its worth. It has been employed partly on routes involving narrow roads and stiff gradients where trams would be dangerous, and partly on other routes the natural beauties of which are so pronounced that it was generally felt that the laying of tramway lines, or the creation of any permanent blots such as are occasioned by the erection of standards and wires, would be altogether a desecration.

The motor omnibus, after passing through its novitiate, has proved in the most practicable possible way the advantages of road motor transport to the general public. It has hit the short distance traffic of railways very hard, and has compelled these latter in self-defence to inaugurate motor services of their own, especially in country districts not well fed by the railways themselves. It is impossible to say to what a great extent the development of motor transport is the result of the anomaly under which the road passenger traffic of London is not controlled by the local governing authorities, who possess in other cities licensing powers reserved in London to the Chief Commissioner of Police.

Other great British cities, as, for example, Manchester and Birmingham, for many years refused to allow the motor omnibus to prove its worth for fear of competition with tramways owned by the municipality, which, being itself the licensing authority, could refuse to give facilities under which any competition with its own concern could come into existence. It is only lately that the prolonged experience of London has proved to all these authorities the enormous utility of the motor omnibus, and its spread to every great city has either become an accomplished fact, or an inevitable development of the near future. Paris, with its smaller fleet of motor omnibuses, has not exerted a similar influence in anything approaching a similar degree throughout the provincial towns in France; and Berlin, which has very nearly tabooed the motor omnibus altogether, has done practically nothing towards the encouragement of motor transport in Germany.

It is rather a curious fact that this policy should have been maintained in Berlin for so long, seeing that for many years past the German Government have been paying huge sums in the shape of subvention, with the sole object of encouraging the national use of trade motors. In all probabilities, the process of ocular demonstration on the streets of the capital would have been more effective than the whole of the expenditure that has been incurred.

From what has gone before, it will be seen that circumstances have all worked together to cause the development of motor transport of Great Britain to be far more rapid than in other countries. Added to this is the undoubted fact that the genius of the British engineer is best expressed in something substantial and durable. The heavy industrial motor is more typical of British tendencies than is the light fast car. As regards the latter we may be good imitators, and may be well able to keep on equality with competition. As regards the former we can do more, and we have shown ourselves able to lead the world and to produce finer industrial motors than can be obtained in any other country.

Even the progressive engineers of the United States acknowledge that they must draw their inspirations in this movement from Great Britain, and are not infrequently to be found in this country studying what has been done, and learning lessons which they will apply at home and which may serve to bring them into strong competition with us, but are very unlikely to make them our superiors.

The general result of all these influences has been, as already stated, that Great Britain is the only European country in which the industrial motor is, in times of peace, used in numbers greatly in excess of the possible military requirements of our own forces. Consequently, the problem before our War Office has not been to encourage the use of heavy transport, but to direct the tendencies of design and popular taste into the channels in which they could be made to fall into line most completely with military requirements.

Next after ourselves, France is fortunate in the possession of the best road system of any European country, and this has helped industrial motor development to progress with fair rapidity, though not at such a speed as to enable the country to be self-supported as regards its needs in military-motor transport. Germany, with a less complete road system, involving in many parts very severe gradients, has had more difficulty still in filling its military requirements, while Austria is in a position somewhat akin to that of Germany from this point of view. Consequently, in all these three great countries, the subvention scheme has had to be rather a scheme for encouraging the use of motor transport of any kind than an attempt to direct designers into any particular channels.

Conditions in Belgium are somewhat akin to those obtaining in France; and, generally speaking, other European countries are so badly served by roads and so unfavourably situated as regards their requirements for the haulage and delivery of goods, that the development of industrial motor transport on a large scale has been out of the question, and consequently, the establishment of any subvention scheme would have proved futile. We are now in a position, with a fairly clear conception of the conditions obtaining in each of the countries concerned, to consider in more detail the nature of the schemes evolved in the interests of military transport, and to ascertain how far those schemes have been brought to successful issues.

CHAPTER 10

British Subsidy Type Motors

In view of the peculiarly advantageous circumstances detailed in the previous chapter, the British subsidy scheme is from the pecuniary point of view less imposing, and from the practical point of view far more comprehensive than any other scheme yet attempted elsewhere. The British War Department favours in general the use of vehicles intended to carry in active service useful loads of about three tons, but as the machines also have to take four men and a considerable quantity of kit and stores, they correspond to ordinary industrial vehicles of four tons capacity.

There is a parallel, but much smaller, requirement, for 30-cwt. vehicles corresponding to the ordinary commercial two tonner and capable of higher speeds than are desirable with heavier machines. These lighter cars are intended for use behind mobile and fast-moving troops, while the heavier type are for the service of the infantry, and for the carriage of ammunition supplies. In each case, the total amount of subsidy paid is from £110 to £120. A portion of this takes the form of a cash payment when the vehicle is accepted, while the remainder is an annual payment spread over a period of three years, and is conditional on periodical inspection revealing the satisfactory condition of the machine subsidised.

The agreement also provides that in the event of the War Department desiring to commandeer the vehicle in time of war, a very liberal price shall be paid to the owner, this price being of course dependent to some extent on the age of the machine. The correct amount is arrived at by deducting from the first cost of the car a certain regular percentage intended to represent the depreciation in value during every half year of normal service. After this deduction has been made, the resulting figure is increased by an agreed percentage of itself, the final result being that the price paid for any car under about two years old is very near, if not quite equal, to the original first cost.

The first move made in the direction of a subsidy scheme in Great Britain dates back to 1908. At that time it was believed that light steam tractors best filled military requirements, and a number of these were registered, the nominal payment of £2 *per annum* being made to their owners. The industrial petrol vehicle was at this time passing out of its period of probation, and it was not long before the military authorities came to the conclusion that it represented a more useful type, in view of the nature of the particular emergencies against which they were chiefly called upon to guard. The ordinary steam-propelled vehicle was open to certain objections, the principle of which is the fact that its carrying capacity of fuel and water is limited, and the latter must necessarily be replenished at fairly frequent intervals. This is no great drawback in commercial work, but might be a very serious matter indeed in times of war, when men and horses have a prior claim on a possibly limited water supply.

In 1911 a scheme of subsidy for transport and supply motors was authorised, and in view of the fact that no such scheme could be matured until it had been in force for several years, a provisional scheme was temporarily adopted, under which total sums ranging from £38 to £52 were paid to owners of vehicles generally of about three tons capacity. The present subsidy scheme was finally put into force in 1912 after the War Office experts had conferred on many occasions with representatives of the leading manufacturing interests. The main objects of the scheme are plainly stated in the War Office specification as follows:

(1) To make the manipulation and control of all vehicles the same; and:

(2) To minimise the number of spare parts which must be carried in the field, having regard to the number of different makes of vehicles of which the transport columns of the army would be composed.

As to the first of these two stipulations, one would think that there could hardly be two opinions, though in point of fact it has been argued in some quarters that no standardisation of driving control is in any way essential. Such a view one imagines can only be held by those who are personally so fortunate as to have that mechanical knack which allows a man to take charge of any car, however different it may be from those to which he has been previously accustomed, and to drive it with perfect safety and efficiency even at night-time and over unknown and bad roads. We cannot assume that every transport driver possesses this instinct, and we must therefore agree that the object aimed at by the War Department is one which deserves every support. It is, in fact, worthwhile to go into a little detail on this point, in order to show what care has been taken to make everything as easy as possible for the driver.

First, as regards the hand control. The steering wheel must provide for 76° of movement of the front wheels of the car; that is to say, 38° of lock from the normal position on either side. In reaching the maximum lock, two complete turns of the steering wheel must be made. Thus, a driver who is used to getting a certain effect by turning his wheel through a certain distance, will find if he is put on to a subsidy car of another make that the same effect is still produced by the same amount of movement. This, of course, helps to make him immediately a safe driver in traffic or at sharp corners. The four-speed change-speed gear is operated by means of a lever in a gate. This gate must be formed of two slots and two selectors, the reverse being a continuation of the first speed slot.

The hand-brake lever must be arranged to push on, and must be well away from the change-speed lever and to the right of it. Furthermore, the brake lever must be 6 inches longer, and must have a plain cylindrical handle, whereas the change-speed lever is finished off with a circular knob. Thus, any confusion between these two levers in sudden emergency, or in the dark, is completely prevented. The throttle and ignition levers must be placed underneath and to the right of the steering wheel, their movement being independent of any movement of the steering column. Increased engine speed must in each case be produced by moving the levers forward. The total movement must be 90°, and the handles must be at right angles to the main axis of the vehicle when in the centre of their travel.

This, again, means that a driver who is accustomed to producing a given effect upon his engine by a given movement of the ignition or throttle is in no way confused by being put on to a different car. The only point in which any variation in driving control is permitted is in regard to the accelerator pedal, the presence of which is optional. However, if a foot accelerator is provided, it must be so combined with the hand throttle that on releasing the accelerator, the throttle valve returns to the position set by the hand lever. The clutch- and foot-brake pedals are marked C. and B. respectively, and the clutch pedal must be on the left, the brake pedal on the right, the travel in each case being about 3½ inches. From these details it will be seen how carefully every item in the driving control has been considered, with a view to facilitating the work of drivers who may have to be moved frequently from one machine to another. As to whether the arrangement adopted is a good one, we have strong evidence of a favourable character in the statement of Mr. J. E. Thornycroft, to the effect that his firm has adopted the War Office system of control as a standard for all their vehicles whether of subsidy model or not.

At a rather later date it may be well worth while to consider whether experience has not demonstrated the possibility of combining with a full subsidy scheme a modified scheme insisting only on vehicles of the right load capacity, and the adoption of all details of the standard control. In this way, if the true subsidy model continues to be somewhat unpopular amongst commercial users, a very fairly adequate reserve will be brought into being without any considerable trouble.

Turning now to the second of the two main points which the War Department have attempted to cover, we find the fulfilment of the scheme beset with much greater difficulties. Every attempt to secure standardisation in the parts of vehicles of different makes must necessarily entail expenditure by the manufacturers, both in getting out new designs and also in arranging for economical workshop processes. Such expenditure is only justified commercially if the sale of the resulting products is sufficient to secure profitable trading. Some allowance, of course, must be made for the added prestige accruing to a firm licensed to build for the War Office, but this is in itself insufficient encouragement. Consequently, every stipulation made with a view to standardisation must be covered by subsidy grants, sufficient to cover both manufacturer and user in respect of any additional cost or disadvantages in operation.

The War Department has recognised the impossibility of asking for complete standardisation, and so killing the individuality of different types of vehicle. The tendency of any such process would be to throttle normal competition, and to prevent progress. Consequently, standardisation can only be attempted in certain respects where it appears for one reason or another to be highly desirable. For example, radiators are notably liable to damage, and consequently the connections of the radiator to the machine are standardised to allow of ready replacement of this essential as a whole. The radiators are mounted on trunnions, the bearings of which are in halves, and the positions and dimensions of inlet and outlet connections are definitely fixed. As an additional safeguard, a stout cord in the form of a bar or tube has to be placed across the front of the radiator. The engines are not standardised except in certain details, as, for example, the method of fastening on and driving the magnetos, which are arranged with a view to rapid removal and replacement whole. No high degree of standardisation is possible without incurring great expense and other disadvantages so far as concerns the design of the clutch and the change-speed gear, though the ratios of the latter are determined for reasons which will be explained later.

As regards final drive, some degree of standardisation is possible so far as the axle arms and bushes are concerned. The bearings of the front wheels are standardised so as to make the wheels interchangeable, and the diameters of both the front and rear wheels are fixed. Makers and users are left with a fairly free hand as regards the type of body to be fitted to a subsidy machine, but in general this must be a lorry body with detachable sides and ends at least two feet high, and carrying a frame to take a complete overhead cover. Use is also found for a certain number of box vans.

Many provisions are made in the subsidy scheme with a special view to making the vehicles suitable for working in convoy. In the first place, it is stipulated that all engines shall be fitted with governors which shall automatically control their speed to 1,000 revolutions per minute. This prevents drivers from racing their engines and overspeeding their cars when running light, and also determines a definite top speed, which should be almost exactly equal for all subsidy machines, as it were. Coupled with this, are the provisions as regards change-speed gear. The engine governor having limited the speed of the 3-ton type to 16 miles per hour, and the speed of the 30-cwt. type to 20 miles per hour, the next step is to secure that, when road conditions require the use of lower gears, the whole of the vehicles in the convoy will need to change gear practically at the same point, and when on lower gears will run practically at the same speeds.

With this object in view, it is stipulated that the ratio between top and bottom gear shall be about five to one, giving bottom speeds of about three and four miles per hour respectively for the two classes. This provision, taken in conjunction with the stipulated engine dimensions, should secure that every vehicle is capable of tackling a

Saurer Motor Field Kitchen

gradient of one in six on normal road surface whether fully loaded or empty. It will be seen that the point kept in view has been the desirability of arranging everything so that drivers of a large number of machines working in convoy—that is to say, running along the same road at short intervals behind one another—shall not have any difficulty in keeping their proper distance, and so in preventing any risk of collisions. For similar reasons the fitting of a ground sprag is made compulsory. The object of the sprag is to prevent a vehicle from running backward if, for example, the driver misses his gear on a steep gradient.

The fitting is not necessary on ordinary commercial machines, since the brakes will almost certainly hold the car before it has run more than a few yards, but in the case of one vehicle in a long convoy, those few yards may mean a collision with the following car, and a hopeless muddle causing serious delay. In view of the possibility of some one car failing, every chassis has to be fitted with towing hooks at the ends of the side members of the frame fore and aft, so that each machine can, if required, either be towed or tow another, and any "lame duck" will not obstruct the whole convoy, but can be dragged along to some point where it can be towed out of the way, and the rest can be allowed to proceed.

Other points in the scheme have in view particularly the fact that the machines must be required to operate on very bad and possibly on very hilly roads, and may even be needed to make detours across country when roads are destroyed or entirely blocked. The chief points in this connection are the provision of high ground clearance, which must in no case be less than 12 inches, the stipulation as to size of wheels, which are rather larger than usually found on commercial vehicles, and various stipulations ensuring adequate protection of the mechanism from mud and dust. Generally speaking, these provisions constitute one of the principal difficulties in making the scheme successful, principally for the reason that large wheels imply a rather high loading platform, and this is objected to by many commercial concerns on the ground that it makes loading and unloading more difficult.

On the other hand, larger wheels are better for the roads, and consequently it is within the bounds of possibility that trading concerns will presently be compelled by law to put up with their disadvantages. From the point of view of motor users in the Colonies, high ground clearance and large wheels are very valuable and even essential fea-

tures. Consequently, the subsidy scheme works in well with many Colonial requirements, and manufacturers whose machines are accepted
by the War Department probably depend for success of the type to no
little extent upon the likelihood of orders from abroad.

In the interests of the proper guarding of the mechanism from
mud and dust, the experts of the War Department have considered it
necessary to stipulate that all cars must be driven on the live-axle system either through bevel or worm gear. In the first instance, only the
former was accepted, but more recently the worm drive, as exempli-
fied by the products of its pioneers, Messrs. Dennis Bros., has met with
approval. The point to be noted is that the chain drive—which, in the
opinion of many manufacturers and also of many users both at home
and abroad is unequalled for heavy work—is definitely debarred.
Considerable antagonism to the scheme as a whole was thus created,
and one is forced to the conclusion that the reasons for refusing the
chain drive were not solely connected with the question of protect-
ing from mud, but were possibly more concerned with the fact that,
while a chain drive is probably quite as economical in maintenance as
any live-axle drive, it requires rather more frequent adjustments and
attention, and possibly small renewals.

In commercial practice, this consideration carries little or no
weight, but on active service a breakdown is none the less serious because it is caused merely by a breakage to one link in a chain and not
by the entire dislocation of the whole transmission gear. One gathers
that, at the present moment, chain-driven machines are in fact being
used in the service of the British Army, and in the interests of the
success of the scheme in the future, the hope may be expressed that
practical experience will show that any fears as to unreliability of this
type of transmission from the military standpoint will prove entirely
groundless.

When the great war broke out, the position was briefly as follows.
The subsidy scheme had not been in force for a sufficient length of
time to secure through its means the complete fleet required. The
War Department itself owned upwards of one hundred lorries of subsidy type, and a limited number were to be found in civilian service.
Among these, the Leyland, which was the first type accepted for subsidy, was probably the most prominent. It has been necessary, therefore,
to depend not only on a supply of machines of subsidy type, but in
the first instance on the requisitioning of other cars of suitable load
capacity, and more lately on the steady purchase of new vehicles of

types which, if not according exactly to the subsidy requirement, approximate to it sufficiently to secure reasonable facilities for the easy repair and maintenance of the machines of the transport and supply columns, both of our existing Expeditionary Force, and also of the new armies now in course of formation.

CHAPTER 11

Transport Motors of Continental Armies

The French subvention scheme, for reasons already explained, has to be more comprehensive in its financial clauses than that in force in Great Britain. Without going into details, it may be summed up in the general statement that the subsidy paid in respect of a lorry of about 3 tons capacity aggregates about £300, spread over a period of four years.

The French Government have specialised for many years past in machines of this and somewhat lighter load-carrying capacity, and more recently they have made serious and fairly successful efforts to encourage the employment of powerful vehicles in which the engine power is arranged to drive all four wheels, and which can be used either as lorries or as tractors, or as a combination of the two. The genius of the French motor engineer, in the opinion of the writer, expresses itself better in the high-speed touring car than in the industrial vehicle. There are excellent examples of the latter to be found, but the average quality of the products of well-known manufacturers is almost certainly not equal to that of corresponding British firms.

A comparison of the relative importance of the two national industries was possible to those who had opportunities of visiting the Industrial Vehicle Show in London in 1913, and subsequently of inspecting the exhibits in the annexe of the Paris Motor Salon later in the same year. On these occasions, as well as during previous opportunities of watching French subvention vehicles undergoing trial, the writer formed the opinion that in many cases the various features of design in any particular vehicle of French origin are peculiarly unequal.

A German lorry fitted for replenishing the supply of gas Zeppelin Airships.

In some portions of the chassis we find adequate or even unnecessarily great strength; in others, unduly light construction and a certain disregard of details making for safety in operation. In many instances the steering mechanism is unnecessarily exposed, and placed very far forward so as to be liable to injury in the case of slight collision or passage over any considerable obstruction. The chain drive is very popular among French manufacturers. The chains are usually not protected by cases, and in very many instances an attempt is made to obtain through the medium of the chain a very large gear reduction, resulting in the use of absurdly small chain pinions, which will certainly need frequent renewal under the conditions of rough service.

In some instances again, the chains themselves are too light for durability. There is also a certain disregard for accessibility of the engine and clutch, and a tendency to employ pneumatic tyres on vehicles designed for heavy loads which would be carried with far less risk of roadside trouble on a rather more substantially constructed solid-tyred vehicle with a good springing system.

Admitting that the French Government could not stipulate any degree of standardisation until they had first obtained a numerically adequate supply of vehicles, one would have thought it possible at least to do something towards standardising the driving control. In some French subvention models, the hand-brake lever is nearer to the driver than the change-speed lever; in others, the opposite arrangement is adopted. Frequently, both levers are of equal length and almost indistinguishable to the touch, which must make it far more dangerous to put a new driver on to a subsidy car when required urgently for night work.

The French subvention trials have been held annually, usually in the months of August and September, and have not been as a rule of a very arduous character. While accompanying the competing vehicles, the writer has been forced to the conclusion that the object of the authorities was rather to pass for subvention any reasonably efficient machine, than to weed out a considerable number and depend only on the most durable. As a rule, during these trials, the competing lorries are parked at Versailles, from which centre they run out daily over a limited number of routes, generally of a very easy character so far as gradients are concerned.

An interesting and potentially valuable feature of the annual French trials has been the compulsory use on all the cars of a variety of fuels. On some days petrol has been used, on others benzol, and on others again a half-and-half mixture of benzol with denatured alcohol, which latter for practical purposes may be regarded as the same thing as methylated spirits. In this way, the French Government have endeavoured to make themselves at least partially independent of any temporary stoppage in the imports of petrol, though so far as we can see at present no such stoppage is in the least degree likely during the present war. Benzol can of course be produced in limited quantities in this country and in France, and if the emergency arose, the supplies of benzol could be greatly increased at the expense of simultaneously laying up stocks of other products not at the moment marketable.

As regards alcohol, a considerable quantity of beet is grown in France, from which either sugar or alcohol can be produced. As a rule, this beet is used mainly for sugar manufacture, since this is the more profitable method of employing it, but in emergency it could be utilised for the production of a very fair quantity of commercial alcohol, thus, roughly speaking, doubling the available stock of home-produced fuel.

The results of these tests have been, on the whole, very interesting. In almost every case, benzol has given better results than petrol, while the benzol-alcohol mixture has given results in some cases rather better than petrol, and in other cases not quite so good. On the average, the mixture has shown itself approximately equal to petrol, so far as consumption is concerned. By visiting Versailles in the early hours of September mornings when the temperature was fairly low, the writer satisfied himself that the use either of benzol or of the mixture did not constitute any serious difficulty in the way of starting up the engines. Moreover, the general absence of offensive smell or smoke seemed to indicate satisfactory combustion of the fuels.

As to the results of the French subvention scheme, the fact that the regulations have recently been made more severe, and certain restrictions as to horse-power, weight, etc., introduced, seems to indicate that the number of vehicles available at the time of the outbreak of war must have been at least approaching the number estimated as required. The last series of trials were only just over when war broke out. In these trials some sixty vehicles competed, representative of a considerable variety of makes and types, including a small number of Colonial lorries of special design, and one or two tractors. On the whole, the vehicles went through the trials well, and the opinions of experts who were present were all to the effect that great improvement was noticeable in mechanical details as compared with previous years.

Incidentally, it may be mentioned that the big fleet of the Paris General Omnibus Co. forms a very useful and conveniently concentrated supply of substantial cars available either for the rapid carriage of troops, or—by the substitution or conversion of bodies—for the transport columns. Numerically, however, the Paris omnibus fleet falls very far short of that of London, while from the mechanical point of view the vehicles are of heavier construction, and one would imagine less easily handled on narrow and winding country roads.

In Germany, a motor transport subvention scheme was inaugurated in 1908. At that time a limited number of German manufacturers were producing considerable quantities of heavy motor vehicles, more especially for export, but it was becoming evident that some very substantial encouragement would be needed to make the home market sufficiently active to be of any real utility to the War Office. Consequently, a scheme was got out which was openly stated to be "a scheme for popularising the use of mechanical transport," or, in other words, a scheme for persuading business houses to adopt a species of transport which, without government aid, would represent an uneconomical and consequently undesirable feature of an industrial concern.

The German Government decided in favour of heavy motor lorries, capable of carrying 4 tons and hauling an additional 2 tons on a trailer. These trailers, contrary to usual commercial practice, are fitted with rubber tyres, since this addition is found to ease the work of hauling by some 25 to 30 *per cent*. The total subsidy for a subvention train consisting of a power lorry and rubber-tyred trailer amounts to something in the neighbourhood of £450 spread over a period of five years. The choice of a heavy type of vehicle was probably justified by the need for limiting the length of the transport columns destined to accompany enormous armies. At the same time consideration has evidently shown that there are grave disadvantages to the use of such heavy cars, and recent regulations have provided more stringent stipulations as to maximum weight.

When the subvention scheme had been in operation for five years, figures were got out indicative of its results up to the end of March, 1913. During this period 825 army trains were subsidised, namely, 743 in Prussia and the other states whose armies are under Prussian control, and 82 in Bavaria. In addition, some 400 lorries of very similar types were sold in Germany outside the scheme, making about 1,200 trains available for use at that time. Allowing for increase in the interval which has since elapsed, we may perhaps put the total available at the outbreak of war at about 1,600. Captain Davidson estimates that the German Army requires for transport purposes about 2,000 of its trains, but this figure presumably does not take into account the needs of the whole of the *Landwehr* and *Landsturm*.

It is admitted that the normal British Expeditionary Force requires about 1,000 3-ton vehicles, which would correspond in capacity to about 500 of the German trains. Consequently, 2,000 of the German trains would apparently only be about sufficient for an army four times the size of our Expeditionary Force. Similarly, the estimate that France needs about 5,000 vehicles of the 3-ton type apparently does not take into account the complete mobilisation of reserves.

The manufacturing concerns which have figured most largely in the German scheme are the German Daimler, the Büssing, the N.A.G., and the Gaggenau. These four have all been participating in the scheme from the start, and about ten other manufacturers have more recently fallen into line, while in Bavaria only three manufacturers have been building to official requirements. The states the industries of which have enabled the strongest support to be given to the scheme are Brandenburg, Saxony, the Rhine Province, Würtemberg, Westphalia, Baden, and Alsace-Lorraine. No less than 41 *per cent*, of the total machines enrolled are normally used in the brewing trade. In this connection, an official report from Bavaria is rather instructive and amusing:

"There are so many breweries in Bavaria, and these are so densely distributed, that there is no need anywhere to convey beer for long distances. Hence there are practically no vehicles employed."

This seriously expressed implication that beer is the only really essential commodity seems to show that lack of humour which appears to be a national characteristic of the German race.

Next after the brewing interests, but far behind in their practical support of the government scheme, come concerns engaged in the transport of goods for export, followed by those concerned in brick transport, flour manufacture, carriage of building materials, agricultural work, and haulage of iron and steel goods.

In endeavouring to estimate how far the existing fleet meets the requirements of the German Army, we have to remember that it consists, at least partially, of machines that have been in service for several years, and that consequently may not be equal to any long strain under peculiarly difficult conditions. It must be presumed that the German

Government has made provision for the continued manufacture of considerable numbers of heavy motor lorries throughout the war, and has not permitted the leading motor works engaged in this class of production to be too far denuded by the mobilisation of their men.

The Austrian subsidy scheme is along the same lines as that in force in Germany, but favours a lorry of slightly lower carrying capacity, probably in view of the mountainous nature of many of the frontier roads. The total amount of subsidy payable is in the neighbourhood of £360 spread over a period of five years. The scheme was inaugurated some time after those of France and Germany, the first trials being held towards the end of 1911. Certain parts of Austria are well provided with roads, so that there is a fair field for the commercial use of motor transport. A large number of vehicles, not of subsidy type, but no doubt capable of being made useful for light work in time of war, are used for the carnage of mails in Hungary. In the Austrian Tyrol, there are numbers of motor services for the carriage of mails and passengers, but on the whole Austria is probably not very well provided with mechanical transport. Her manufacturing industry is limited, and she imports in fair numbers from her neighbour, Germany.

Italy can only find very small use for heavy motor vehicles in commercial service, and consequently it would be futile as yet for the Government to depend upon anything in the nature of a subsidy scheme. During the Tripoli campaign, a considerable number of rather lightly built lorries were obtained by direct purchase and proved very serviceable. Probably they are not of a type which would be by any means ideal in a European war, though they were doubtless the right thing for work over loose sandy tracks where heavier machines might well have become inoperative.

Russia also has no subsidy scheme on account of its comparatively poor industrial development, and also the very inadequate quantity and quality of its roads. For such vehicles as are used, the country is dependent upon import, while the army must depend solely on direct purchase from foreign manufacturers. It is rather interesting to note that out of about 2,000 industrial motor vehicles exported by Germany during the year 1913, no less than 25 *per cent*, went to Russia, practically the whole of these being known to represent Government orders. Russia has been buying motor lorries for military use from British firms for many years past. An engineer who accompanied one of the first vehicles supplied from this country, describes the roads over which the car had to work during its official trials as follows:

The road was covered with fine sand, banked up a few feet above the level of the surrounding country, in which the wheels of peasants' carts had cut ruts about 12 ins. to 14 ins. in depth. The gauge of these ruts being narrow, it was necessary to drive with one pair of wheels in the ruts, the other pair meanwhile cutting ruts of their own. At intervals planked bridges had to be crossed. These were old and unsafe; therefore, it became necessary to lay down a temporary track of boards to distribute the weight over as many planks as possible.

At first sight it would appear that under such conditions the purchase of motor lorries by the Russian Government represents a waste of money, but the facts are explained by a credible story circulated within a few days of the outbreak of war to the effect that the Austrian military *attaché* a day or so before leaving Petrograd expressed surprise that so many motors were being mobilised.

"Your roads are so bad," he said.

"Yes," was the reply, "but yours are good."

CHAPTER 12

Emergency Measures on the Outbreak of War

A noteworthy feature in connection with the mobilisation of the British Army on the outbreak of war was the energy with which the great motoring organisations took up the duties of rendering the private motorist, so far as might be possible, available for the service of the government. The Royal Automobile Club sent out a circular letter to some sixty provincial Automobile Clubs affiliated to the parent body, asking that their members owning motor cars should be requested immediately to register them with the R.A.C. for the use of the War Office and Admiralty, in case they should be wanted. This scheme was simultaneously furthered by means of advertisements in the principal organs of the London and provincial press, and posters were placed in all the club's officially appointed hotels and garages throughout the Kingdom.

Registration forms asking for particulars of cars, and an indication of the nature of the service for which they would be made available, were rapidly prepared and widely distributed with admirable results. These machines were placed at the disposal of the War Office and Admiralty both for home and for foreign service, and in many cases their owners made their own services available for facilitating or accelerating the urgent business of the country by providing officials with a ready means of rapid transit.

In addition, the club kept in constant communication with the British Red Cross Society, and has put at the disposal of this Society the use of the R.A.C. annexe at 83, Pall Mall, for office, store and organisation purposes. As the need for the provision of motor ambulances for foreign service became urgent, the club gave invaluable assistance to the Society by keeping up a constant flow of cars unreservedly given or lent by their owners. Cars have been supplied for this and other purposes through the R.A.C. organisation from practically every county in England, Scotland, Ireland and Wales. All members and associates of the club have been asked to assist the work of recruiting by carrying on their cars cards urging prompt enlistment.

The Automobile Association and Motor Union was equally energetic and prompt. The Association immediately conveyed to the War Department an offer to help the government to the fullest extent of its resources, and upon the acceptance of this proposal communicated at once with its 92,000 members—owners of cars, light cars, cycle-cars and motor cycles—inviting them to volunteer their services, and to that end to forward the fullest possible particulars. The response to this appeal resulted in the enrolment of the names of about 20,000 motor owners, and within a few days large numbers of these were being utilised not only by the War Office, but by municipal and other bodies all over the country.

The earliest mobilisation took place on the Doncaster racecourse, where about 150 cars assembled in a few hours in response to telegrams. This fleet remained concentrated for some days, but the eventuality against which it was intended to provide did not materialise. Large numbers of the A. A. members were employed during the first two or three weeks of the war to guard telephone and telegraph lines and cables, until permanent arrangements could be made for this service. Hundreds of motor cycle and car members undertook long spells of duty by day or night under the supervision of the post office officials.

In connection with the conveyance of wounded, the Association placed fleets of cars at the disposal of the chief military centres throughout the country, its members holding themselves in readiness to go out at any hour during the day or night, to carry wounded from the railway stations to the hospitals. In a considerable number of cases, the motorists so employed undertook, at their own expense, to convert their cars into ambulances, and a large number of machines so transformed were sent across the channel to work behind the firing line. Vehicles were also forthcoming in plentiful numbers to meet refugees, and take them to their temporary homes.

Hundreds of motorcycle members volunteered for dispatch-carrying work, and the committees of the National Service League and other recruiting bodies in all parts of the country were supported by

One of a fleet of "Maudslay" motor buses commandeered by the War Department, and fitted with lorry bodies

cars, light cars, and motor cycles with side cars, ready to pick up recruits and convey them to the enlisting depots. At normal times, the Association employs on the main roads of the country over 500 road patrols, whose duties involve continual cycling over their appointed beats from daybreak until dark. These men were evidently ideal recruits for the cyclists' battalions required for scouting work. Over 250 of them enlisted in various regiments, or rejoined their old regiments, while a picked body, over 100 strong, was formed into the first two companies of the 8th Essex (Cyclist) Battalion, under the command of the Secretary of the Association, Captain Stenson Cooke, who was formerly a member of the London Rifle Brigade.

The Commercial Motor Users' Association undertook the enrolment of men competent to serve as motor transport drivers, and also formed on behalf of its own members a kind of transport exchange. A similar scheme on rather broader lines was handled by the Imperial Motor Transport Council, the idea being that while some business concerns would experience difficulties in effecting deliveries owing to their horses being requisitioned, others—owing to the disorganisation of trade—would have suitable facilities standing idle. In that event considerable trouble might be saved by bringing into existence some machinery capable of establishing contact between the two groups.

The council also undertook work in assistance of the Motor Ambulance Department of the British Red Cross Society, and circularised its oversea members with a view to assisting the maintenance of British export trade in motor vehicles.

At the outbreak of war, steps were immediately taken by the War Department to secure for service all the motor lorries of subvention type working for commercial houses. These not being numerically sufficient for the whole needs of the army, several thousand other motor lorries of approximately the same carrying capacity, but of varying types, were requisitioned somewhat hastily. The quality of the fleets thus formed was variable, even though a process of weeding out at the ports of embarkation did something towards securing uniformity.

In the same way the urgent need of employing many thousands of transport drivers naturally led to the enlistment of men of varying capabilities. Drivers handling lorries or 'buses are in some instances required to be fairly capable mechanics. In others, any interference with the mechanism of their machines is discouraged, and they are taught to be entirely dependent on the mechanical staff at their headquarters. Such men, while thoroughly skilled in handling a vehicle, are

A LARGE NUMBER OF DAIMLER LORRIES HAVE BEEN TAKEN OVER BY THE MILITARY AUTHORITIES. THE EXAMPLE SHOWN IS FITTED WITH A SHIELD CONTAINING A SHEET OF TRIPLEX GLASS WHICH WILL STOP A RIFLE BULLET AT 100 YARDS.

not really fully qualified for the business of a motor transport driver in active service.

Very considerable numbers of London motor omnibuses were taken off the streets and converted into ambulances or lorries, and similar vehicles have also been used for the transport of troops and other purposes.

As soon as matters had had a little time in which to settle down, it became apparent that the government did not intend to rely on the system of requisitioning to make up the wastage of their fleet in service, or to provide transport for Indian and Colonial troops, or for the new armies in course of formation. For this purpose large regular orders were placed with many of the leading manufacturers, and in some instances these orders amounted to taking over practically the entire output. No exact figures are available as to the rate at which, during the early stages of the war, the government took delivery of new motor lorries, but there is little doubt that the weekly supplies ran into three figures, and that a continuance of very substantial orders will be necessary right up to the conclusion of hostilities.

In European countries, the comparative shortage of industrial motor vehicles rendered necessary a more wholesale programme of requisitioning. Thus, for example, Paris was promptly denuded of the whole of its fleet of motor omnibuses, about 1,100 in number. A few years ago, the old double-deck type of motor omnibus, at one time used in Paris, was discarded in favour of a long-bodied single-decker, capable of carrying up to about forty passengers. These machines are so designed to the requirement of the government as to be capable of being transformed rapidly into waggons for the carriage of meat. The windows are replaced by wire-gauze screens, the seats removed and the handrails fitted with hooks. Alternatively, the 'buses can be equally easily adapted for the carriage of wounded, by simple fittings from which stretchers or hammocks can be slung.

During mobilisation, numbers of motor vehicles were employed in France to transport troops, and, moreover, those of the Paris 'bus type are of undoubted utility for this purpose whenever it may become necessary to transfer moderately large bodies of men rapidly from one point to another, where convenient railway communication does not exist.

All the Continental countries involved in the war made strict provision against the export of motor vehicles of any kind, while even in Great Britain an order was, for a period, in force, prohibiting the export of heavy industrial vehicles. It was, in fact, realised in advance in all quarters that a war of such magnitude and involving the employment of such huge numbers of men, could not conceivably be fought along the lines anticipated and subsequently realised, unless full dependence were placed upon motor transport in the first case for the provision of food supplies, and as a corollary for a similar service of warlike stores, for the carriage of wounded, for scouting, and for enabling commanders and staff officers to travel with sufficient rapidity and freedom to make it possible for them to realise with sufficient accuracy the essential facts with which they were called upon to deal.

"Get There!"

(Extract)

Contents

"Get There!"

It may be said, without taking undue liberties with the truth, that the newest branch of the American Army, the Motor Transport Corps, owes its existence to a Mexican bandit named Francisco Villa, sometimes called "Pancho" for short. You may have heard of him. Though the officers who wear on their collars the insignia of the wheel and the winged helmet will probably disagree with this statement, asserting that their corps is an outgrowth of the Great War, it is, nevertheless, a fact that the present huge organisation, which controls all the motor-driven transport of the American Army, had its beginning in the handful of trucks, barely a score in all, which ploughed their way across the sands of Chihuahua in the wake of Pershing's little punitive column.

When Villa and his raiders swooped down upon the border settlement of Columbus on the night of March 8, 1916, there was not a single organised motor-truck unit in the army, our officers, most of them trained in the schools of Indian and Filipino warfare, insisting that no motor-driven vehicle was as sturdy and dependable as the old-time escort wagon and its four-mule team. The refusal of our staff authorities to recognise the advantages of motor transport is the more difficult to understand when it is remembered that for close on four years there had been unfolding before our eyes the countless object-lessons of civil life and of the war in Europe, every highway from the North Sea to the Alps being crowded with the motor-driven vehicles of the fighting armies.

The present Motor Transport Corps, (as at time of first publication), may be said to have been born when, three days after the Columbus raid, General Funston, in command of the Southern Department, telegraphed to Washington for authorisation to form a number of motor-truck companies for service with the punitive expedition.

The War Department acted promptly. The request was immediately approved, and within three days twenty-four trucks had been purchased, a force of civilian drivers had been recruited, and the entire outfit loaded aboard special trains. As soon as the trains reached Columbus the trucks were loaded with supplies and sent across the border to overtake the expedition, which was already well into northern Mexico.

Notwithstanding the total absence of anything resembling roads, despite the deep sand, the extreme heat, and the inexperience of the drivers, the trucks caught up with the column before the supplies which it had taken from the United States were exhausted. From that moment the value of motor-driven vehicles for military' purposes was firmly established in the minds of American officers, even the most hidebound old Indian fighters, who disapproved of everything new on principle, being compelled to admit that the mule must give way to the motor.

The first two motor-truck units proved so extremely efficient that the organisation of others was begun, and by June 30 there had been formed fifteen companies in all. The personnel of these early motor-transport companies was civilian, the drivers and repair men being provided by the factories which supplied the trucks, but it quickly became apparent that the employment of civilians would not prove satisfactory because of their lack of discipline and the consequent difficulty of keeping them under control, the officers not knowing how to handle civilians. So, whenever possible, enlisted men who had had experience with motor vehicles or who possessed some mechanical aptitude were transferred to the truck companies to replace the civilians, the latter remaining on to give instruction in driving and maintenance.

Maintenance is, I might add, perhaps the most important factor in the successful operation of motor vehicles, for broken-down cars must be repaired, worn parts must be replaced, and the vehicles must frequently be overhauled. In order to maintain in a state of efficiency the truck trains operating in Mexico, it was found necessary, therefore, to build repair-shops and to organise repair crews. Though the personnel of these shops, like the drivers, was at first largely civilian, it, too, was gradually replaced by enlisted men, so it may be said that by the opening of 1917 motor transportation had become a recognized branch of the military establishment, although it was not until some time after declaration of war that it was authorized for the army.

Although, upon our entry into the European war, preparations were immediately begun for the complete motorization of the various trains—ammunition, engineer, sanitary, and supply—which comprise the divisional trains, each of these sections was still controlled by the corps or department to which it pertained. In other words, the ammunition trains were controlled by the Ordnance Department so far as the procurement of vehicles and the supply of personnel was concerned; the engineer trains were under the control of the Corps of Engineers; the sanitary trains were under the Medical Corps, and only the supply trains came under the jurisdiction of the Quartermaster Corps. It must be understood, however, that the divisional trains were assigned to and became a part of the division itself, being, therefore, under the direct command of the divisional commander.

As might have been expected, this system resulted in inefficiency and confusion because of municipal officers in control. Instead of all motor activities being directed by a single head, each of the staff departments using motor vehicles had its own ideas and worked along its own lines. Thus, the Corps of Engineers had designed and was manufacturing various types of vehicles adapted to engineering work. The Signal Corps was producing vehicles designed for carrying radio equipment, photographic laboratories, and the like.

The Medical Corps was experimenting with various types of ambulances, dental wagons, and mobile laboratories, while the Ordnance Department was dividing its allegiance between the tractor type and the model known as the "Quad" or four-wheel drive. Thus it was that for many months after the declaration of war the motor activities of the army were distributed among several arms of the service, with the inefficiency and duplication of effort which invariably results from decentralization.

The necessity for a separate organisation to handle motor transportation was first recognized by the A. E. F., and in December, 191 7, General Pershing issued a general order creating a Motor Transport Service. The new service was described as a part of the Quartermaster Corps, and an assistant to the Chief Quartermaster was detailed as its chief. For all practical purposes, however, it became a separate organisation. In the United States the transition was more gradual, it not being until August, 1918, that the Secretary of War authorized the creation of a Motor Transport Corps as a separate and distinct branch of the military establishment. Colonel Charles B. Drake, who was later made a brigadier-general, being named as its first chief.

The new organisation was built up along the same lines as the Motor Transport Service, the officers and men of the latter being transferred to similar positions in the new corps, thus enabling them to continue the performance of their duties without interruption or confusion. The effect was as though the Motor Transport Service was lifted bodily out of the Quartermaster Corps, renamed, and made completely independent, the only visible sign of the change being, however, that the officers and men changed their Quartermaster insignia for the winged helmet superimposed upon a motor-wheel which was adopted as the device of the new corps.

Under the new order all the motor transportation of the army, save only tractors used for artillery purposes, was embraced in the Motor Transport Corps. The Medical Corps, the Engineer Corps, the Quartermaster Corps, the Signal Corps, and the Department of Military Aeronautics, all of which had developed special types of vehicles for their respective needs, immediately turned over their equipment to the new organisation. The designing of bodies was left to the several branches, but the designing of all types of chassis was included in the functions of the Motor Transport Corps.

Among the duties of the new corps were the design, procurement, storage, maintenance, and replacement of all motor vehicles, though a few weeks later procurement was assigned to the Purchase, Storage, and Traffic Division of the office of the Quartermaster-General, with the proviso, however, that the Motor Transport Corps should prescribe the type and design of the vehicles supplied to it. The corps was thus enabled to insist that it be supplied only with the standardized military truck, the design of which had been achieved by the Motor Transport Service in spite of much opposition and after untiring effort. This arrangement also effectually prevented the purchase and use of vehicles of many different designs and put an end to the complicated and extravagant system of spare parts and supplies inseparable from the use of a multiplicity of types.

I might mention, in passing, that in the spring of 1917, just prior to our entry into the war, the automotive engineers of the United States met in Washington and, putting aside all thought of commercial rivalry or profit, or, indeed, of everything save patriotism, designed a motor-truck which combined the best features of the many trucks which were then being manufactured, placing at the disposal of the government designs and patents that were the result of heavy expenditures of time, money, and talent. This work of standardisation was in charge of Mr. Christian Girl, who was probably better fitted for the task than any man in the United States. The result was a standardised military motor-truck which is generally admitted to be the most efficient vehicle of its kind in existence.

The efficiency of any motor-transport service, no matter how well equipped with vehicles, must depend primarily upon the efficiency of its personnel. The finest truck that mechanical genius can design and money can buy can be ruined in a few hours by the carelessness or ignorance of its driver. It was quickly realized, therefore, that, if the Motor Transport Corps was to give efficient service, its officers and men must be as carefully trained as their fellows in the combatant branches of the army. The first real training-school for Motor Transport officers was established by General Pershing in France, its students being recruited mainly from Americans who had gone overseas prior to our entry into the war and had entered the French service as camion and ambulance drivers.

These men possessed much practical knowledge, gained in actual warfare, and a large percentage of them were given commissions in the Motor Transport Service of the A. E. F. The chief training-centre in the United States was at Camp Joseph E. Johnston, on the St. John's River, near Jacksonville, Fla., and a smaller one was later organised at Camp Meigs, in the District of Columbia. Using as a basis of instruction the curriculum adopted by the A. E. F., the officers and men at these camps were given a very thorough course of training in all phases of motor-transport work, including road-training, tactics, maintenance and repair of cars, and a certain amount of infantry drill in order to inculcate discipline. But with the growth of the army increased training facilities became imperative, it being estimated that between 20,000 and 30,000 men per month would be required by the Motor Transport Corps.

In fact, requirements from overseas for men for operations up to July 1, 1919, was placed at upward of 231,000 officers and men. In order to train these men and organise them into the proposed units, it was planned to establish motor-transport training-centres at Camp Bowie, Texas; Fort Sheridan, Illinois; Camp Fremont, California; Camp Wheeler, Georgia, and Camp Taylor, Kentucky, which, in conjunction with the schools already in operation at Camp Joseph E. Johnston and Camp Meigs, and other schools which had been established by the Committee of Education and Special Training, would have given a total monthly training capacity of 23,800 men. The signing of the

Armistice put an abrupt end to this enormous training programme, but plans have already been perfected for the formation of a Motor Transport Reserve Corps, which, it is believed, will result in providing a large number of officers trained in motor-transport duties and ready for immediate service in the event that the United States should again go to war.

About six weeks before the signing of the Armistice a spectacular campaign was inaugurated in order to obtain for the corps recruits possessing the necessary technical and mechanical training. Officers and civilians were sent to the principal cities in the United States to open recruiting offices, though no funds were appropriated for office rent, clerical hire, supplies, or advertising, each recruiting officer being expected to exercise his ingenuity in procuring all of the above without cost to the government. But thanks to the co-operation and assistance rendered by the local Chambers of Commerce and Boards of Trade, and to the patriotism of the automobile manufacturers and newspapers, the campaign proved, in spite of the lack of funds, a remarkable success, there being received more than 50,000 applications for enlistment.

Shortly after the beginning of hostilities steps were taken toward the establishment of three great motor-transport centres: Camp Holabird, about twenty miles from Baltimore, on the shores of Chesapeake Bay; Camp Jessup, at Atlanta, Ga., and Camp Normoyle. The huge assembly and repair shops erected at these camps are perhaps the most complete plants of their kind in existence, being of permanent construction and adapted to the needs of the army for many years to come. At each of these camps storage facilities have been provided for the vast number of motor vehicles which will not be required under peace conditions, but which will be kept in constant readiness for use in an emergency. Practically all motor vehicles destined for service overseas passed through Camp Holabird, where they were uncrated, assembled, put in thorough running order, inspected, registered, and finally loaded aboard ship for transport to France.

During the last summer of the war, when the shipment of motor vehicles was at its height, Camp Holabird was worth journeying a considerable ways to see, there being literally acres of vehicles, ranging all the way from huge artillery repair trucks, veritable machine-shops on wheels, to "flivvers" which unsuccessfully attempted to conceal their identity beneath coats of olive-drab. The paint-shops were, incidentally, one of the most interesting features of the camps, the paint being sprayed on the vehicles by means of air-brushes and a hose in little more time than it takes to tell about it. Thanks to this ingenious method, it did not take very much longer to paint a motor car or a truck than it does to polish a pair of shoes.

Then there were the trimming-shops, where tops, curtains, boots, and cushions were turned out by the thousand; the supply depots, whose huge steel and concrete buildings were stacked to the ceilings with incredible quantities of tires, tubes, lamps, and other accessories; the repair-shops, with their forges, lathes, and travelling cranes; and the spare-parts department, where, thanks to a remarkably ingenious card-index system, there could be obtained without confusion or delay any duplicate part that might be called for, whether it was a new rear axle for a mobile repair-shop or a tiny cotter-pin for a motorcycle. Though these great shops had been in operation only a few months when the war ended, and though their personnel had been obtained anywhere, everywhere, almost at a moment's notice, they were probably, everything considered, the best organised and most efficient plants of their kind in the world.

The Motor Transport Corps naturally resolves itself into two main branches: Park Service and Field Service. The first of these branches is subdivided, in turn, into four general types of parks: Reception, Organisation, Replacement, and Repair. The Reception Park was usually established at, or near, a base port for the purpose of receiving motor vehicles for shipment abroad. Here the vehicles were uncrated, assembled, registered, and put in running condition. This done, the vehicle was sent on to an Organisation Park, where vehicles and men first met, the latter coming from one of the Motor Transport Corps schools; here the various units were organised, and the personnel and material held in readiness for assignment.

The function of a Replacement Park is, as its name signifies, to fill any deficiencies in equipment or personnel. Though this scheme of organisation was quite generally adhered to in the A. E. F., each camp in the United States devoted to motor-transport activities may be said to have combined the functions of Reception, Organisation, and Replacement Parks under a single head.

The present organisation of the Field Service units of the Motor Transport Corps is, (as at time of first publication), as follows: the personnel of a motor-transport company consists of a first lieutenant, a second lieutenant, eight sergeants, forty-four privates (ten first-class), and two cooks; the equipment consists of a light open motorcar, a

MOBILE MACHINE-SHOP OPERATING IN A VILLAGE UNDER SHELL FIRE.

SUPPLY OF MOTOR TYRES.

A MOTORCAR WRECKED RETURNING FROM THE FRONT LINE.

motorcycle with side-car, twenty-nine cargo trucks, including one for light repair and one for company supply, two tank trucks, and a rolling kitchen. A motorcycle company has a first lieutenant, a second lieutenant, six sergeants, a corporal, thirty privates, first-class, and a cook, together with thirty-two motorcycles with side-cars, and two cargo trucks. A headquarters motor command is in charge of a captain, who has two first lieutenants, a second lieutenant, five sergeants, four corporals, and two privates, first-class; the rolling-stock includes two heavy motor-cars, two light closed cars, one light open car, one cargo truck, and two motorcycles with side-cars. Though there are no tables of organisation for the larger units of the Motor Transport Corps, a Supply Train is composed of a headquarters motor command and not less than two or more than six motor-transport companies.

So much space has been devoted in the newspapers and magazines to the exploits of the combatant arms of the service that the public has heard little, if anything, of the less spectacular but no less arduous and important work of the men who wore the purple hat-cords of the M. T. C.

It was their endurance and resourcefulness which made possible the transfer by road to the St. Mihiel and Argonne sectors, in nineteen days, of more than half a million men, and this in spite of the unprecedented congestion as a result of the preparations in progress for the great offensives. It was the tireless, iron-hard drivers of the M. T. C. who got forward the food for the men and the food for the guns. It was the despatch-riders of the corps who, jeering at death, delivered the vital messages which were entrusted to them, tearing down the steel-swept, shell-pocked roads at express-train speed on their roaring motorcycles. No mud was too deep, no shell-storm too violent, no road too dangerous to stop the men of the M. T. C.

They went wherever their wheels could find traction—and in some places where they could not. They did not possess so much as a bowing acquaintance with either fatigue or fear. They were the newest corps in the army and they made their own traditions. They were as unconventional in their methods of doing things as the old-time army teamster, the stage-coach driver, and the pony-express rider, whose qualities they have inherited and whose lineal descendants they are. When in doubt they stepped on the accelerator, for the motto of the Motor Transport Corps is "*Get There.*"

"Treat 'Em Rough!"

(Extract)

Contents

"Treat 'Em Rough!"

It is rather a curious circumstance that the idea from which was evolved one of the most formidable weapons of the war, and one which proved a prime factor in bringing Germany to her knees, was obtained by an Englishman in Germany, from under the very noses of the Germans themselves, who did not have the vision to recognise its amazing military possibilities. About a year before the Teutonic wave surged across the frontiers of France, the representative of a California manufacturing concern was giving demonstrations in the larger German cities of a singular device known as the Holt caterpillar tractor. Though this contrivance, in spite of its grotesque and clumsy appearance, could cross ditches and surmount obstacles with amazing agility, it did not arouse particular interest among the Germans, for it was intended for the pursuits of peace, whereas they were even then seeking new means for making war. But it chanced that among the onlookers at one of the demonstrations was an English traveller, who had the imagination to see in the clumsy machine, as it waddled across an apparently impassable terrain with the relentlessness of fate, something more than an agricultural appliance.

Upon his return to England he described the tractor to Colonel E. D. Swinton, who evinced the liveliest interest in the subject, closely examining the pictures and asking countless questions. I might add that General Swinton, for he has since been promoted, has, unlike most professional soldiers, a highly developed imagination, as is shown in the stories he has written, the best known of which is entitled *The Green Curve*. Colonel Swinton, who had served in the South African campaign, had long had in mind an idea for an armoured fighting-machine, a sort of small fort on wheels, which could be propelled by its own power over ground impassable to any other type of vehicle. The caterpillar tractor gave him the means of propulsion which he had been seeking. But, as might have been expected, the hidebound, brassbound officials of the War Office condemned the suggestion as fantastic and impractical, it not being until 1915, when the gloom of despondency overhung the land and people snatched at straws of hope, that Swinton's plans were taken from their pigeonhole for reconsideration and he was reluctantly given permission to show what he could do.

Upon caterpillar tractors brought from America he proceeded to mount armoured hulls built according to his own designs, the land battleships thus created being armed with both field and machine guns. They were tested under conditions of the greatest secrecy, the trials proving so successful that the construction of a considerable number was immediately authorised. In order that the public might obtain no hint of the true nature or purpose of these terrible new weapons they were referred to as "tanks," the impression being given that they were intended for transporting water. Painted in dull colours and swathed in tarpaulins, fifty tanks were landed at Le Havre on August 29, 1916, and were moved up to the Somme front under cover of darkness. At dawn on September 15, everything being in readiness for the launching of the great Somme drive, they were entered in battle on a most astonished foe.

Though I saw one of the tanks in action on this occasion—it was named, if I am not mistaken, "*Crème de Menthe*"—I was not permitted to photograph it or to write about it. It has repeatedly been asserted that these tanks were the first vehicles of their kind in the history of warfare, and that is true, so far as the method used for their propulsion is concerned, yet it is interesting to note that, ten years before the Great Navigator set foot on the beach of San Salvador, Leonardo da Vinci had written as follows to the Duke Ludovico Sforza:

> I am also building secure and covered chariots which are invulnerable, and when they advance with their guns into the midst of the foe, even the largest army masses must retreat, and behind them infantry may follow in safety and without opposition.

Everything considered, the tanks were not of much assistance to the infantry on the occasion of their first appearance, though they unquestionably caused considerable consternation in the German lines. Owing to delay in production, the British were obliged to employ at the Battle of Arras, on April 9, 1917, tanks identical with those which had been used on the Somme and which were, in reality, fit only for training purposes, having only 8-mm. armour. Nevertheless, two battalions were launched on a two-kilometre front, and there is no doubt that they rendered valuable service, the capture by twelve tanks of a German stronghold known as "The Harp" being a particularly noteworthy achievement.

Eighty-eight tanks of an improved model, protected with 12-mm. armour, were used in the attack on Messines Ridge, June 7, 191 7, but the success of the infantry was so complete on that occasion that the tanks had only an unimportant role to play. The torrential rains which fell during the early stages of the Ypres offensive on July 31 turned the battlefield into a broad and treacherous morass, in which tanks were of but little use. The following figures, which were doubtless as well known to Hindenburg as to Haig, explain why the tanks did not sweep everything before them, as it was confidently expected that they would do, and why the Germans were no longer particularly alarmed by their appearance:

	Battle of	Tanks in action	Ditched	Hit by shells
First day's fighting..	Arras	60	33 (55%)	7 (2%)
	Messines	88	7 (19%)	4 (5%)
	Ypres	133	60 (45%)	37 (28%)

It was my understanding at the time that the use of tanks by the British during the fighting on the Somme caused great annoyance to the French High Command, it being asserted that the British had agreed not to make use of their machines until the tanks which the French had under construction were ready, when both armies would make a combined tank attack on a large scale. How much foundation there was for this assertion I do not know, but perhaps it was as well that the British tanks made their debut when they did, for the French did not make use of tanks until April 16, 1917, when 132 Schneider tanks attacked between Rheims and the Aisne. A French report reads:

> In spite of the congratulations of the commander-in-chief, the results did not meet expectations, although wherever tanks were used they led the infantry beyond the advance of the rest of the front of attack.

It would seem that it was not until the British victory at Cambrai, when 430 tanks were used to lead a large attack, in the course of which 8,000 prisoners and 100 guns were taken, that the German High Command realized that the use of tanks could no longer be postponed, for shortly thereafter the German Tank Corps was formed, an Antitank School of Instruction was established, and orders were placed for a large number of antitank rifles. The Germans experienced numerous manufacturing difficulties, however, in the construction of their tanks, and when Marshal Hindenburg inspected the first fifteen *panzerkraftwagens*, as they were called, at Charleroi, in March, 1918, he damned them with the faint praise: "They probably won't be of much use, but since they are made we might as well employ them."

This discouraging send-off apparently had its effect, for the original of the *Elfriede* type—*Elfriede* herself—was ditched and captured near Villers-Brettoneux a few weeks later. By contriving to unite in this one model all the faults of the British and French tanks, the Germans once again proved the truth of the old saying: "*Success has many imitators, but sometimes they copy only her defects.*" According to a German deserter, the German Tank Corps in July, 1918, consisted of 25 German tanks and 50 repaired British machines.

This same authority stated that 250 light tanks had been ordered for delivery in September, 1918, and that in April construction had been begun on a monster 38 feet long, weighing no tons, carrying four 77-mm. cannon and 13 machine-guns. This formidable war-engine, called a "*Fahrbarer Sefechtsunsterstand: ver dunden mit Artillerie unt Infanterie Beebachtung,*" boasted contrivances for creating artificial mists (probably similar to our own smoke-producing devices), for laying and covering its own telephone-wires *en route,* was equipped with wireless, and carried a crew of an officer and twenty-eight men. If this super-tank was ever constructed, it certainly never went into action.

The Germans were more successful, however, when it came to devising protective measures against tank attacks. These consisted of trenches of peculiar construction and design, some of them from 15 to 20 feet wide and 6 to 8 feet in depth; "tank traps," consisting of deep pits with camouflaged covers; bridges so built as not to support a tank's weight; mine-fields; special tank observation-posts; *Tank Goschutz Batterie,* as the Germans called their groups of 77-mm. antitank cannon; 55-mm. tank batteries, which were kept in pits about a thousand metres from the front line and were only brought up when tanks were signalled; trench mortars mounted for horizontal fire; machine-guns firing armour-piercing bullets; hand-grenades with concentrated charges, and antitank rifles.

The antitank rifle was a single-shot Mauser, mounted on a bipod, weighing 32 pounds and firing an armour-piercing ball of 13-mm. calibre. At close range this weapon penetrated the British heavy and the French light tanks. Had it been used in groups it might well have proved extremely formidable, but the unpopularity it enjoyed because of its heavy recoil combined with a well-founded reluctance on the part of its users to await the near approach of a tank, in a large measure neutralized its effectiveness. Toward the close of the struggle it seems to have fallen into general disuse, and when the Armistice was signed the enemy was preparing to supplant it with a 22-mm. machine-gun, a few of which had already been used with considerable success.

When the United States entered the war in April, 1917, the value of the tank as a weapon of offense had been so thoroughly established that steps were immediately taken to form a tank organisation of our own, a special regiment—the 65th Engineers—being raised for the purpose. The units of this regiment were recruited at Camp Upton, New York; Camp Devens, Massachusetts; Camp Meade, Maryland; Camp Lee, Virginia, and Camp Cody, New Mexico, the entire regiment being assembled in March, 1918, at Camp Colt, on the battlefield of Gettysburg, which then became the general concentration and preliminary training-camp for the tank organisation. The tanks passed from the control of the Corps of Engineers on March 6, 1918, when the Secretary of War directed the organization of the Tank Corps as a separate arm of the service, Lieutenant-Colonel Ira C. Welborn, a regular infantry officer, being commissioned as colonel and appointed director of the Tank Corps in the United States.

The structural organization of the corps, as it existed at the close of the war, consisted of General Tank Headquarters, with 15 officers and 60 men; Army Tank Headquarters (one for each field army), with 7 officers and 27 men; Brigade Headquarters, 4 officers and 47 men; a Heavy Battalion, with a strength of 68 officers and 778 men; a Light Battalion, consisting of 20 officers and 375 men; a repair and salvage company, 4 officers and 146 men; a Depot Company, 4 officers and 138 men. To each Army Tank Headquarters were assigned 5 brigades, each brigade being composed of 3 battalions, 1 heavy and 2 light, and 1 repair and salvage company. A battalion consists of three companies, each company having three platoons. As five fighting-tanks are assigned to each platoon, it will thus be seen that a field army has 675 tanks at its disposal.

The commissioned and enlisted personnel of the Tank Corps was of as high an average, both mentally and physically, as any organization in the army, not even excepting the Air Service. About 65 *per cent* of the corps were technically trained men—engineers and machinists—while the remaining 35 *per cent* was composed of business and professional men, farmers, cow-punchers, college undergraduates, and soldiers of fortune. They came from every section of every State in the Union. Their versatility was denoted by the pipings of their overseas caps—blue, red, and yellow—which denoted that they combined the functions of infantry, artillery, and cavalry.

Several other colours might appropriately have been added, however, for the tank men were as familiar with Browning, Lewis, and Vickers as the machine-gunners, they knew as much about gas-engines as the Motor Transport Corps, they were as competent to make repairs as the men of the Ordnance Department, and in action they took as many risks as the youngsters on whose breasts were embroidered the silver wings. They were as keen as razors and as hard as nails. They were, to use the phraseology of the plains, fairly "rarin' to go," and they were ready and anxious to fight at the drop of the hat. In fact, that was why they joined the Tank Corps—because they believed it offered more opportunities for Boche-killing than any other branch of the service.

The training of the tank units was based on infantry drill, which is the best means of instilling discipline. This was supplemented, however, by instruction in the use of machine-guns and tank cannon and in the operation and maintenance of gas-engines, the men finally being brought to a point where they were ready to take up technical and tactical tank training at the British and French tank-training centres, to which they were sent as soon as there was accommodation for them. Thousands of men, trained to the limit of the facilities in this country, were held at Gettysburg from April and May until August and September because of the shortage of tanks and the lack of training facilities in France.

Not until September, in fact, did any tanks become available for training purposes in the United States, when there arrived five British heavy tanks and several light tanks of American manufacture, thus permitting training to be resumed on a larger scale. When the Armistice was signed, the Tank Corps had a total of 20,212 officers and men, of whom 8,183 were serving in Europe. Shortly before the collapse of Germany preparations had been begun for the great Allied drive planned for the spring of 1919, steps being taken to increase the corps to a point where it could supply tank units for four field armies. The proposed strength for this purpose was 57,940 officers and men, it being planned to have this entire force fully organised, trained, equipped, and in France by the early spring of 1919.

The programme of tank construction for the American Army was initiated in February, 1918, but, owing to the extensive arrangements which had to be made with numerous manufacturers for the enormous number of parts required, and to the fact that there existed in the United States little or no accurate data regarding tank construction, the first light tank was not delivered to the Tank Corps in the United States until the following September. Owing to the more complicated mechanism of the heavy tanks, none of them was completed before the signing of the Armistice. The machines used by the American Tank Corps units engaged on the Western Front were supplied by the French and British, no American-built tanks being employed in active fighting during the war.

After a series of conferences between American, French, and British tank officers, it was decided that two types of tanks should be manufactured in the United States: a heavy model (Mark VIII) and a light machine (Mark I) known as a "whippet." The heavy tank, which weighs thirty-five tons and carries a crew of one officer and nine men, is armed with two six-pounder rapid-fire guns and six Browning machineguns, and is capable of a speed of from four and one-half to six miles an hour over ordinary ground. The whippet, named after a breed of small dog used in England for racing, was an adaption of the French Renault tank. It weighs six tons and carries a crew of two men—a driver and a gunner—and over ordinary ground can move at a speed of from seven to eight miles an hour. These, then, were the two types of tanks originally decided upon, but, as will be seen, the programme was considerably altered.

When it was decided that the United States should embark on a programme of tank construction, the Ordnance Department had only the haziest instructions to guide it. Owing to the mystery in which the French and British enshrouded the details of their tank construction, all that our Ordnance officers knew about a tank was that it should be able to cross trenches at least six feet wide, that it should be protected with armour-plate approximately five-eighths of an inch thick, and that it should carry one heavy gun and two or three machine-guns. Two experimental machines were laid down and work started on them at once, these models being intended to develop the

THE AMERICAN WHIPPET TANK.

THE MARK V TANK.

A Squadron of Whippet Tanks Advancin
in Battle Formation.

A Squadron of Whippet Tanks Parked and Camouflaged to
Conceal Them from Enemy Observation.

possibilities of the gas, electric, and steam systems of propulsion as well as to ascertain the relative advantages of very large wheels and a specially articulated form of caterpillar tread.

At this time the British were using and were interested in a large tank only. The French had been using a medium-sized tank, known as the Schneider, but, as it had not been wholly successful, they had developed a much smaller two-man machine, called the Renault, which presented some very decided advantages and which they eventually adopted as their only type. While the large British tank had been reasonably successful in operation, it had certain very decided limitations which the British themselves recognised, so, after a thorough investigation of its possibilities and shortcomings, it was decided to redesign the large tank rather than to copy the existing model with its admitted defects.

It was furthermore decided that the work of designing should be done jointly by British and American engineers, acting under the Anglo-American agreement drawn up as the result of a conference at British General Headquarters, which provided for the joint production by England and the United States of 1,500 large tanks, England to furnish the hulls, guns, and ammunition, the United States to provide the power-plant and driving mechanism. When the Armistice was signed, approximately 50 *per cent* of the work represented by the American components had been completed, and it was confidently expected that the entire programme of 1,500 would have been completed by March. England had about 250 of the hulls ready when the Armistice was signed.

The work of manufacturing the French type of tank had not progressed satisfactorily, however, this being partly due to the delay involved in changing all drawings from the metric system to the American, and to the difficulty which was experienced in inducing American concerns to take on the production of this machine, which is extremely complicated and difficult to manufacture. It was necessary, therefore, to divide up manufacturing activities on this tank between a considerable number of plants. The original programme called for 4,440 of these small tanks, of which 209 had been completed by the end of December, 1918, with 289 more partly completed and production just getting under way. There was every reason to believe that the entire number would have been ready for use by April, 1919.

During the last summer of the war two new types of tank were developed. One of these was a two-man, three-ton affair, which the Ford

Motor Company guaranteed to produce at the rate of one hundred a day. Orders were placed with that concern for 15,000 of these "flivvers" and the first 500 machines would have been ready for delivery on January 1, but upon the signing of the Armistice their production was stopped.

The other machine was a successor to the French Renault, but designed with a view to quantity production. It carried three men instead of two and was armed with both a 37-mm. cannon and a machine-gun, whereas the Renault carried only two men and one weapon. The cost of production would have been very much less than the Renault machine and the weight substantially the same. One thousand of these had already been ordered and negotiations were pending for a second thousand—the first to be delivered in January and the entire two thousand by the end of March.

In addition to the above activities, the Ordnance Department had decided to build 1,450 of the large Mark VIII tanks, including hull, guns, and ammunition, entirely in this country. In fact, work on the interior components for this lot of machines was well under way when the Armistice was signed.

It was perhaps as well for the Germans that they contracted yellow fever when they did, for had the war continued long enough to permit of America launching the avalanche of tanks which she had under construction, the Huns certainly would have had heart-failure. I doubt, indeed, if any Americans, save the handful of officers directly concerned, realise how tremendous was our tank programme. When the war ended, orders had actually been placed for 23,390 tanks, representing an outlay of approximately $175,000,000.

This vast fleet of tanks was to be manned by some 58,000 men— as many as there were in the entire American Army prior to the war with Spain. *Had these tanks been placed side to side they would have formed a moving wall of steel forty miles long.* Even the comparatively few Tank Corps units which had an opportunity to get into action gave the enemy a taste of what we were preparing for him. Their crest was an angry cat. Their motto was "*Treat 'Em Rough!*" And they did.

The Dennis 30 cwt. Chassis

Contents

ESTABLISHED IN 1895,
MESSRS. DENNIS BROS., LTD.
ARE KNOWN THE WORLD OVER,
IN AUTOMOBILE CIRCLES,
AS THE ORIGINATORS OF THE WORM GEAR.

THE TIMES, MARCH 7TH, 1913

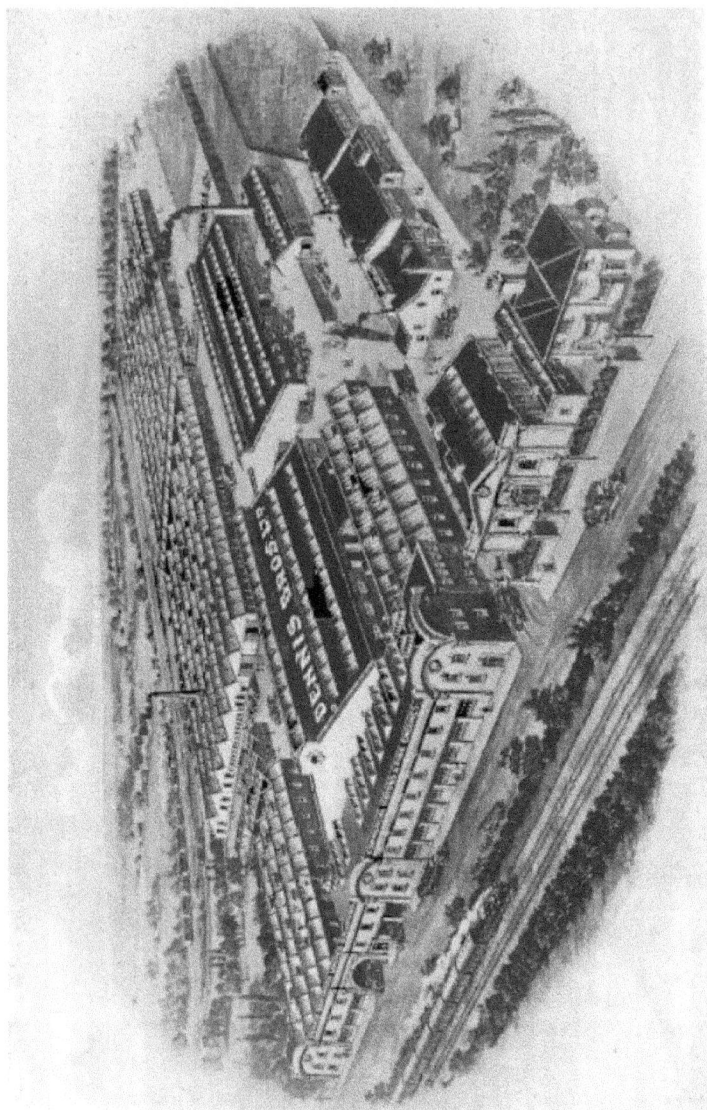

MESSRS. DENNIS BROS.' GUILDFORD FACTORY.

The Dennis 30 cwt. Chassis

Nothing succeeds like success and that obtained with Dennis vehicles is almost phenomenal. For many years there have been no more popular chassis, for they have borne the test of time, giving wonderfully efficient service, combined with low running cost, in many cases after ten, and even more, years of active life.

As long ago as 1913 *The Times* said:—

> To a very great extent Great Britain owes her pre-eminence in commercial motorcars to the foresight, energy, and resource of the firm of Dennis Bros., Ltd of Guildford. Established in 1895, Messrs. Dennis Bros., Ltd., are known the world over, in automobile circles, as the originators of the worm gear. They were the pioneers of this remarkable invention, which has revolutionized the motor industry, at a time when experts unanimously declared that they were wrong. They stuck to their opinion and their sound judgment is now proved by the almost universal adoption of the innovation.

In introducing our 30 cwt. chassis, we would like to emphasize that this entirely new model has been by no means hastily produced; many of its features are the result of very careful and prolonged tests and experiments carried out in the factory, and on the road, and, to quote another authority, it may be said of this as of all other Dennis models that the chassis is a "representation of ripe experience accumulated over thirty years of sound work."

A large number of these chassis have been in operation for goods and passenger service, both at Home and Overseas, for the past two years, and the experience thus acquired under the most exacting road conditions has been duly noted and turned to good account by those responsible for the final design.

Our aim throughout has been to evolve, not a cheap machine, but one that should combine all that is best in high-class engineering practice—in a word, to produce a machine that will give "no-trouble" service under all working conditions. Thus, while pneumatic tyres are optional wheel equipment, the chassis has been constructed throughout to withstand the effects of shocks and vibrations experienced when running continuously over indifferent road surfaces with solid-tyred wheels.

At the same time, very careful attention has been paid to the question of unladen weight, and the use of the highest grade material has, in spite of its sturdy construction, ensured a light chassis. The weight of the complete chassis, with lighting set, is only 29 cwt., fitted with pneumatic tyres.

In conformity with usual Dennis practice, the importance of ease of maintenance has been constantly borne in mind, and not only are all parts requiring occasional attention easily accessible, but dismantling of the main components can be effected with very little trouble.

This applies particularly to the engine, clutch, and gearbox, which unit can be easily detached from the chassis. Then, again, the driver's duties in looking after the machine are rendered as light as possible, grease-gun lubrication being provided throughout the chassis, whilst the illustrations will show that the importance of a good general appearance has not been overlooked.

To produce, at a popular figure, a vehicle that has been built up to a standard and not down to a price called for very extensive manufacturing facilities, and an installation of the most modern machinery and plant, and these conditions exist in a very high degree at both our Guildford and Coventry factories, where the workshops cover an area of 25 acres.

An essential feature of such a programme is that there must be standardization; consequently every part of the Dennis 30 cwt. model, like the larger Dennis chassis, is made to jig, which ensures perfect accuracy of all parts and absolute interchangeability.

Not only first outlay, but running costs, have been the subject of much consideration, and, with a view to improving petrol consumption, we have adopted a four-speed forward gearbox. The change speed lever is carried on the side, as not only are we convinced that this is the best position, but it also possesses the practical advantage, in the case of passenger vehicles, of allowing an extra passenger to be accommodated on the front seat.

The petrol and oil consumption during exhaustive trials, on average roads, was 20 miles per gallon of petrol, and 800 miles per gallon of oil. With the chassis weight of 29 cwt., body weight 10¾ cwt., driver, spare wheel and tools 3¼ cwt., and a net load 30 cwt, the aggregate gross weight of the vehicle was 3 tons 13 cwt., which gives a fuel consumption figure of 73 ton miles per gallon.

The running speed of the lorry on these trials was 23-25 miles per hour, but there is no difficulty in obtaining 33 miles per hour on the level with a full load.

The powerful 85 m/m bore x 120 m/m stroke engine, which develops 30 h.p at 1,500 r.p.m., will enable the vehicle, with a full load, to climb a gradient of 1 in 4¾ on reasonably good-surfaced roads.

The excellent results of the practical tests to which the many vehicles on the road have been put during the past twenty-four months, enable us to place the new 30 cwt. model in bulk production in the fullest confidence that its reliability and all-round efficiency will be at least up to the high standard of other Dennis productions.

We offer this new chassis with our reputation behind it, and supported by the prestige that has accrued to us, as the pioneers of the worm drive, and the first firm successfully to adopt the turbine pump to motor fire engines.

The full specification which follows will well repay careful study.

CONSTRUCTIONAL DETAILS OF THE DENNIS 30 CWT. CHASSIS

Engine—Four-cylinder type, cast *en bloc*, bore and stroke 85 by 120 m/m; developing 30 h.p. at 1,500 revs, per minute, and 35 h.p. at 2,000 revs, per minute. The valves are all placed on one side, and the valve stems, together with the adjustable tappets, are enclosed by an oil-tight cover which can be removed for the purpose of adjustment. The cylinders and top half of crankcase are cast in one piece, while the cylinder head is detachable. The engine, clutch and gearbox are built up in one unit, and suspended from the main frame at three points, thus ensuring flexibility and preventing any lack of alignment.

The complete unit is easily detached from the chassis. Lubrication of the engine is carried out by a pump driven from the camshaft. The oil is carried to and distributed by the hollow camshaft to the main crankshaft bearings. The crankshaft is drilled to allow the oil to be led direct to the connecting-rod bearings, and the overflow from these bearings lubricates the piston and gudgeon pin bearings by splash. The filler for the oil tank and the "sight rod" oil gauge are both on

AN EXAMPLE OF ATTRACTIVE COACHWORK ON A 30 CWT. DENNIS CHASSIS.

A THREE-QUARTER FRONT VIEW OF THE DENNIS 30 CWT.
CHASSIS, AS SEEN FROM THE OFFSIDE. THE CURVED RADIATOR AND
TAPER BONNET GIVE THE VEHICLE VERY ATTRACTIVE LINES.

the same side of the engine.

Ignition—Ignition is by high-tension B.T.H. magneto. The timing is variable by hand control, and the complete magneto is easily detachable.

Carburettor—Automatic type, fed from a 10-gallon petrol tank. The control of the carburettor is carried out by hand from a control lever under the steering wheel, and by foot from the usual type accelerator pedal.

Water Circulation—After a careful trial with the Thermo-Syphon system, it was decided to adopt the water pump circulation as being much superior, especially in hilly and in tropical countries. Provision is made for draining all water from the system for winter conditions.

Clutch—The clutch is of the external cone type, faced with fabric. It has three external springs, very accessible and easily adjusted. An adjustable clutch-stop is provided.

Gearbox—The gearbox is arranged to give four forward speeds and reverse. The fourth speed is direct, and the standard ratios are—fourth, 1 to 1; third, 1.63 to 1; second, 2.82 to 1; first, 4.6 m to 1; reverse, 3.94 to 1. The gears are controlled by a side change speed lever, the mechanism being provided with a positive locking device which prevents two gears being meshed at the same time. The main gearbox shaft runs on ball bearings, while the secondary shafts run on roller bearings. The gears are of 6/8 pitch, and are of such width as to ensure long service, the material being chrome nickel steel. The shafts are of large diameter, splined to take the drive from the gears, and are made as short as possible in order to prevent deflection.

Unit—The engine, clutch-housing and gearbox are bolted up to form a single unit, which is very rigid, and which at the same time allows great accessibility. The big-end bearings can be examined and adjusted by taking off the oil sump, and the gearbox by removing the top cover which carries the change speed mechanism. The gearbox can be taken down as a unit, after removing the propeller-shaft and brake connections, and the clutch itself forms a self-contained unit which can then be removed.

Torque Tube—The torque tube is provided with a spherical head which not only takes the driving torque and the brake reaction from the rear axle, but also takes the thrust necessary to propel the vehicle. The tube, with its flange at one end, is all made in one piece, and is of

THE NEARSIDE OF THE POWER UNIT, SEEN FROM THE FRONT,
SHOWING THE TAPPET COVERS THAT ENCLOSE ALL THE VALVE
STEMS, THE ACCESSIBILITY OF THE PUMP,
MAGNETO, AND CARBURETTOR.

THE DENNIS 30 CWT. CHASSIS, AS SEEN FROM THE REAR.
NOTE THE LARGE DIAMETER REAR BRAKES, DETACHABLE
POT AXLE, BALANCED ARBOUR SHAFT WITH SPHERICAL
HEAD, STURDY CROSS MEMBERS, ETC.

large diameter. Tapering from the rear axle to the ball end, it encloses the tubular propellershaft which transmits the drive from the universal joint at the back end of the gearbox to the worm.

Front Axle—The front axle is an "H" section stamped from special steel and heat treated. The swivels are fitted with ball thrust bearings. The front road wheels are fitted with taper roller bearings, which can be adjusted to take up any slight amount of wear which may develop after continuous use.

Steering Gear—The steering gear is of the Ackerman type. It is operated by a worm and wheel placed in an oil-tight case supported from the frame. Provision is made that, if any wear takes place, it can be re-meshed in a fresh position. The cross steering connection has ball joints provided with grease-gun lubricators, while the connection to the steering gearbox has spring-loaded ball-joints, each of which is adjustable for wear and provided with grease-gun lubricators.

Wheels—These are hollow spoke cast steel, for cushion tyres. Pneumatic tyres are fitted to detachable pressed steel disc wheels, which are held in position by 8 bolts provided with spherical seated nuts.

Tyres—The standard fitting is Cushion (Dunlop or other makes), 34 in. (1 10 m/m for 720 m/m front and 140 m/m for 720 m/m rear, rim fitting). Pneumatic tyre sizes (straight-sided Dunlop) are 33 in. by 5 in. front and 34 in. by 7 in. rear. With the pneumatic tyre equipment is supplied one spare detachable disc wheel fitted with a cushion tyre 34 in. (110 m/m for 720 m/m rim fitting), as well as a brace spanner and a rim operating tool. The cushion-tyred wheel acts as a spare for either the front or rear wheel.

THE ENGINE, CLUTCH AND GEARBOX OF THE 30 CWT. CHASSIS FORM A SINGLE UNIT, HERE SHOWN IN A THREE-QUARTER VIEW TAKEN FROM THE REAR. THE LARGE DETACHABLE COVER OPENS UP THE GEAR-BOX AND CLUTCH FOR INSPECTION.

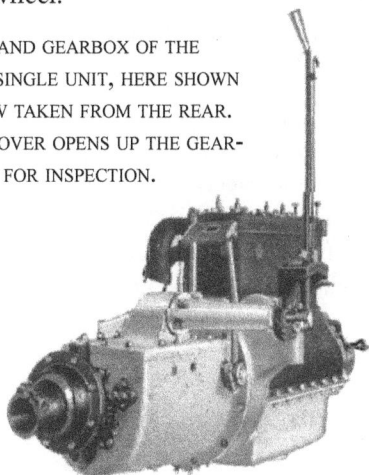

Frame—The frame is of pressed steel channel section, provided with pressed steel cross members.

Back Axle—The axle is contained in a steel casing which carries the whole weight of the vehicle. The power is transmitted to it through special high-efficiency Dennis worm gearing. The top cover of the steel casing is easily removable without taking down the axle or the wheels. When removed, it carries with it the worm and wheel and the differential gear. The live axles themselves can be easily withdrawn without removing the wheels or jacking up the chassis. An oil filler is fitted in an accessible position at the back of the axle casing, and enables the oil level to be easily ascertained. The rear wheels run on hardened and ground bearings, which are fitted with gunmetal floating bushes.

Brakes—Both the foot and hand brakes are lined with asbestos fabric, and are of the internal expanding type, acting on 16 in. diameter brake drums bolted to the rear hubs. Special provision is made to prevent grease from finding its way on to the brake surfaces. Cams are used to expand the brake shoes, and adjustment can easily be made by means of large adjusting nuts which are placed in an accessible position at the rear end of the brake pull rods.

Road Springs—These are of special design. The rear springs are 3 in. wide and allow for ample deflection, and the front springs are 2 in. wide and are also very flexible, thus ensuring absence of vibration while the vehicle is travelling on bad roads. The spring shackle bolts are all provided with grease-gun lubricators.

Petrol Consumption—18-20 miles to the gallon.

Oil Consumption—One gallon to 800 miles.

Equipment—Each chassis is equipped with a Lucas electric lighting set, consisting of two large commercial type electric head lamps, 2 side lamps mounted on the wings, and tail lamp, wired up to accumulator and lighting dynamo; electric horn; the usual roll-up kit of tools; front mudguards and step; lifting jack; speedometer and mileage indicator, driven positively from the rear of the gearbox. Provision is also made for fitting a self-starter and a mechanically-operated tyre pump at a slight extra cost.

CHASSIS PARTICULARS

Length overall	16 ft. 7 5/8 in.
Width overall	5 ft. 7 3/8 in.

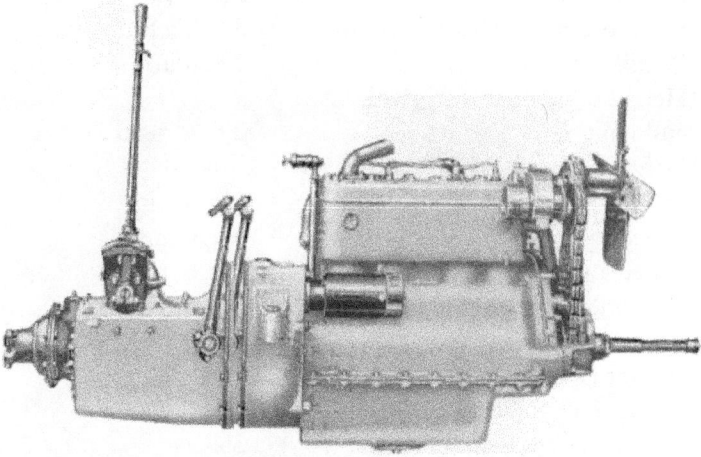

A VIEW OF THE OFFSIDE OF THE POWER UNIT, SHOWING THE FAN AND
DYNAMO WITH THEIR "V-BELT" DRIVES, AND THE ELECTRIC SELF-
STARTER.

SHOWING SOME OF THE PRINCIPAL CASTINGS OF THE ENGINE. LEFT TO
RIGHT—TIMING GEAR CASING, CYLINDER BLOCK (WITH VALVES
ASSEMBLED) AND CRANKCASE, TAPPET COVER, AND SPECIALLY
DESIGNED DETACHABLE CYLINDER HEAD.

Dash to end of frame	12 ft. 9 in.
Dash to centre of back axle	8 ft. 8½ in.
Width of frame	2 ft. 6 in.
Height of frame loaded (with cushion tyres)	2 ft. 47/16 in.
Height of frame loaded (with pneumatic tyres)	2 ft. 4¼ in.
Wheelbase	1 ft. 0 in.
Wheel track	4 ft. 8 in.
Ground clearance under rear axle	105/8 in.
Turning circle (approximately)	40 ft.
Weight (approximately)	29 cwt.
Body weight (allowed for)	10¾ cwt.
Driver, spare wheel, and tools	3¼ cwt.
Load	30 cwt.
Total gross weight	73 cwt.

THE STANDARD 30 CWT DENNIS BOX VAN
SPECIFICATION OF STANDARD BOX VAN

The framing is constructed with well-seasoned selected English ash and oak, strengthened with forged and malleable iron corner plates and brackets. Roof of tongued and grooved yellow deal covered with special roofing canvas. Double doors at rear hung on special improved pattern hinges.

Body panels in silver finish 22-gauge steel. Sundeala or armoured three-ply birch. Interior fitted with the necessary casings and linings for panel protection.

Floor of tongued and grooved yellow deal with iron wearing strips.

Ample room and comfortable seat for driver and roundsman, with hair-stuffed cushion and back rest.

Two-piece windscreen, top portion to open outwards.

Painted grey, ready for final painting and lettering.

Height inside body on centre line (floor to underside of hoop shield) 5 ft. 6 ins.

Length inside body, 8 ft. 3 ins.

Width inside body, 5 ft. 6 ins.

Width of rear doorway, 4 ft.

Height of rear doorway, 5 ft.

Cubic capacity behind the driver's seat, 240 cubic feet.

SIDE VIEW.

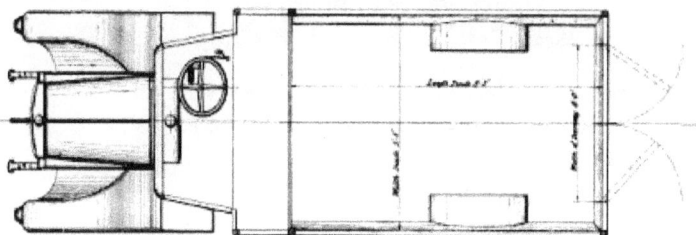

SECTIONAL PLAN.

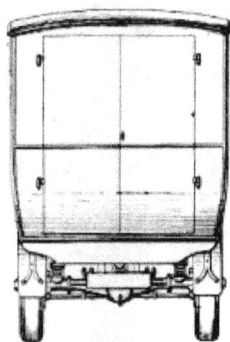

REAR VIEW.

STANDARD BOX VAN ON 30 CWT. CHASSIS

A STANDARD BOX VAN BODY MOUNTED ON A
30 CWT. CHASSIS, FITTED WITH CUSHION TYRES.

FRONT AND REAR, END-ON, VIEWS OF THE STANDARD
BOX VAN LORRY, ILLUSTRATED ABOVE.

DENNIS 30 CWT. TIPPING LORRY

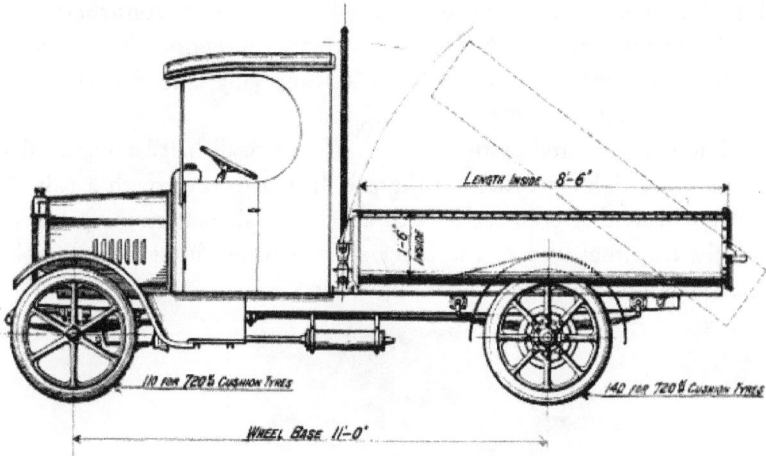

ELEVATION OF 30-CWT. TIPPING LORRY, SHOWING ANGLE OF TIP.

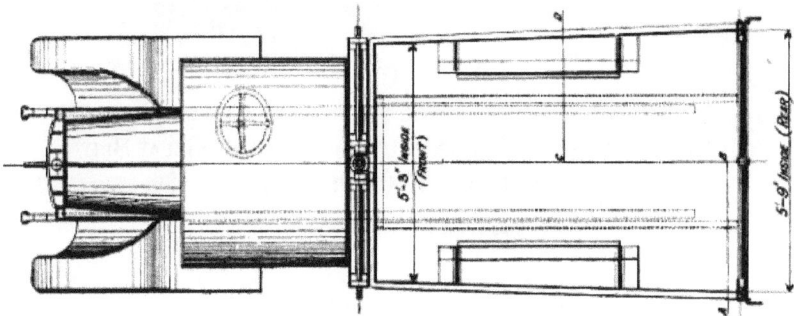

PLAN OF TIPPING LORRY. NOTE THE TAPERED BODY,
TO FACILITATE UNLOADING.

In the above illustrations a steel body is shown, with wheel arches, in order to secure a low loading line. The bodywork of the Standard Tip Wagon is of wood, and without wheel arches. Its construction is similar to the Lorry Body (below) with the exception that it tapers outwards towards the rear, to facilitate emptying, and that the tailboard, only, is hinged, the sides being fixed.

The body is tilted by the rotation of a vertical shaft having a substantial thread, located behind the cab. It is driven through a pair of bevel wheels that connect it with a horizontal shaft running transversely. To either end of the latter shaft may be fitted a detachable crank-handle, easily operated by one man.

30 CWT. STANDARD HINGE-SIDED LORRY FITTED WITH CUSHION TYRES. THE CO-OPERATIVE SOCIETIES OF GREAT BRITAIN OPERATE OVER 1,000 DENNIS VEHICLES.

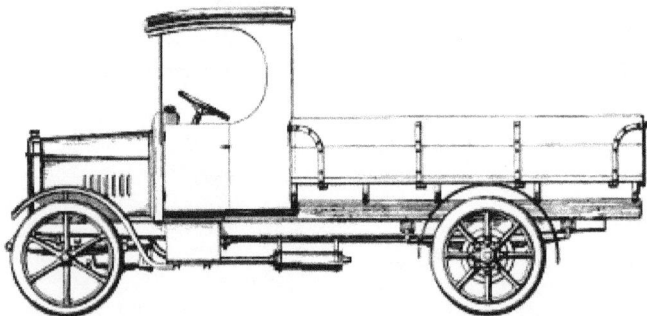

DRAWING OF STANDARD 30-CWT. HINGE-SIDED LORRY FITTED WITH CUSHION TYRES. SIDE VIEW.

Specification of 30 cwt. Lorry Body

Framing in selected and well-seasoned English ash and oak. Sides of British Columbia or Oregon pine. Floor of tongued and grooved yellow deal. Half-round iron wearing plates on floor, also on top edge of sides and tailboard.

Sides can be made fixed or hinged, and detachable. Tail board hinged and also detachable.

Cab has ample room and comfortable seat for driver and roundsman, with hairstuffed cushion and back rest, and window in rear.

Ironed up with mild steel forgings and pressings.

Two-piece windscreen, top portion to open outwards. Painted grey, ready for final painting and lettering.

Body measurements—

Length inside	8 ft. 6 in.
Width inside	5 ft. 6 in.
Height of sides	1 ft. 6 in.
Cubic capacity to top of sides	2¾ cub. yds.
Approximate loaded height of platform	3 ft. 4¾ ins
Wheel base	11 ft. 0 in.
Wheel track	4 ft. 8 in.

The 16-Seated Dennis Saloon Bus

This Saloon Bus has seating accommodation for 16 passengers.

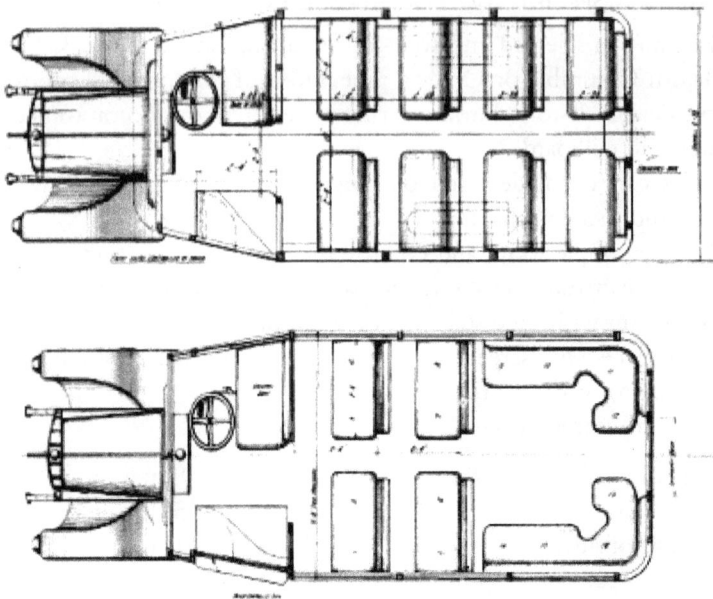

PLANS OF ALTERNATIVE SEATING ACCOMMODATION IN THE 16-SEATER BUS.

THE 19-SEATED DENNIS SALOON BUS
BRIEF SPECIFICATION OF 16-19 SEATED SALOON BUS BODIES

Pillars, rails, cross-members and runners are of dry selected ash and oak.

Exterior panels of 22G steel, rear corner panels beaten to shape, and interior panels constructed of three-ply birch.

Floor of ¾ in. red deal, tongued and grooved. Inspection traps fitted over gearbox and rear axle.

The outer roof is supported on ash hoopsticks, having a camber of 9 in., strengthened with mild steel brackets and plates. Roof boards of spruce or B.C. pine.

All main windows glazed with sheet plate glass, and two on each side can be made to drop, if required, in which case they are provided with necessary spring balances and anti-rattle devices.

A half partition, glazed in the upper part, divides the coach behind the driver.

Front entrances with sliding door give access to the bodywork. Emergency door at rear.

Driver's screen extends up to, and is fitted to, overhead canopy

160

THE SALOON BUS, ILLUSTRATED ABOVE, WILL ACCOMMODATE
19 PASSENGERS SEATED.

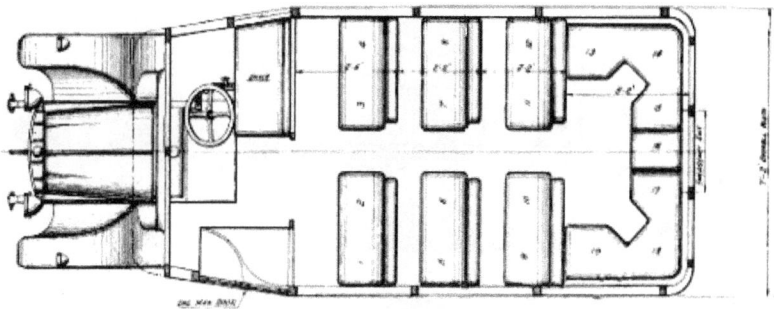

SEATING PLAN OF ABOVE BUS.

extension.

All upholstery in moquette or leather cloth. Seat backs covered to match, also inside of omnibus up to height of seats. Bracket on offside of driver's seat to accommodate the fire extinguisher.

The whole mounted on the chassis, fitted with mudguards, and painted in first-class coach style to any approved colour.

STANDARD 16-SEATED MOTOR COACH BODY

BRIEF SPECIFICATION OF STANDARD 16-SEATED MOTOR COACH BODY

Framing of selected and well-seasoned English ash and oak. Bottom tongued and grooved yellow deal; heel boards and seat framing of American cotton wood.

Doors to all seats on near side and to off side of front seat, fitted with slam lock and rubber silencers.

Dennis patent hood (Patent No. 1773) which is exceptionally easy to put up and down, with all-weather side curtains.

Steps covered with linrubber and brass edging.

Leather upholstery. Spring cushions, and backs hair stuffed.

Windscreen in three pieces, top portion to open outwards.

Filled up, rubbed down, painted and varnished to any approved colour in the best coach style.

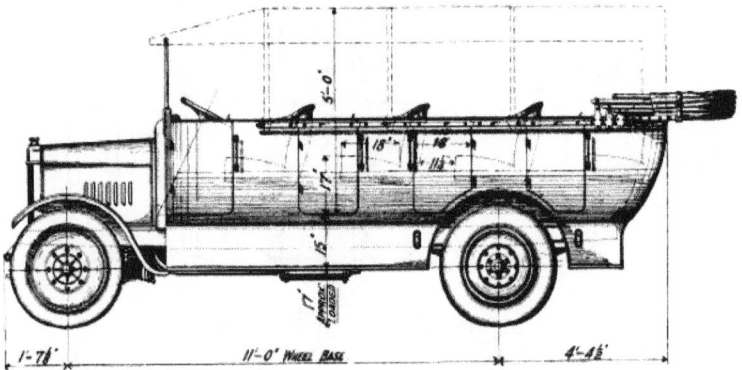

SIDE VIEW.

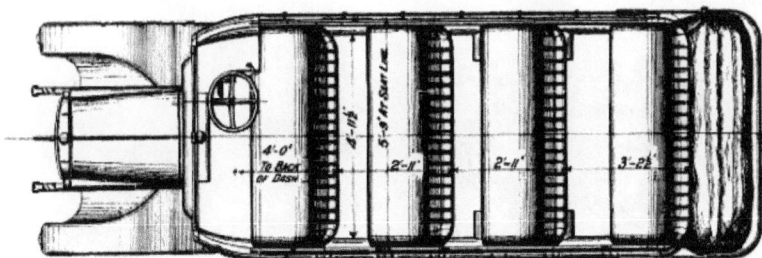

PLAN VIEW.

FRONT VIEW.

THE STANDARD 16-SEATED DENNIS COACH

THIS PHOTOGRAPH SHOWS HOW COMPLETELY THE PASSENGERS ARE
PROTECTED FROM THE WEATHER BY THE COMBINATION OF HOOD AND
SIDE-SCREENS ON ALL DENNIS MOTOR COACHES.

"WE THINK, AS OUR COACH IS ONE OF THE FIRST TO BE FITTED ON THIS CHASSIS, YOU WILL BE INTERESTED TO HEAR THAT THE MACHINE HAS GIVEN EVERY SATISFACTION, AND IS VERY POPULAR WITH OUR PASSENGERS. WE EXPECTED—AND HAVE OBTAINED—THE SAME RELIABILITY FROM THE SMALL COACH AS WITH OUR LARGER DENNIS MACHINES."—A. HARRIS, ESQ., PARK GARAGE CO., COVENTRY.

THE DENNIS AMBULANCE

DENNIS AMBULANCE IN THE SERVICE OF THE LAMBETH BOARD OF GUARDIANS.

REAR VIEW OF AMBULANCE, SHOWING ARRANGEMENT OF INTERIOR.

BRIEF SPECIFICATION OF AMBULANCE BODY

Local Government or similar type of body, of the best selected ash and oak framing with mahogany panels, or aluminium.

Two doors at rear, opening outwards, to give full clearance for stretchers. Two plate-glass embossed panels at each side; look-out window in the back door; ventilators in sides and roof.

Two stretchers, one above the other; top stretcher to be slung and run on a folding frame covered with stout canvas, with pillows complete.

Seat (tip-up) inside for sitting cases and attendant.

Windscreen; driver's cab with door at each side.

Provision for accumulators and tools; first-aid box inside.

Driver's and inside seats upholstered and spring cushions.

Floor covered with lino.; waterproof roof; spare wheel attachment; mudguards, lamps, brackets, number plates, etc.; rear folding step; illuminated sign. The whole painted to choice.

COACHBUILDER DRAWINGS AND DIMENSIONS OF
THE 30 CWT. DENNIS CHASSIS

SIDE VIEW OF CHASSIS

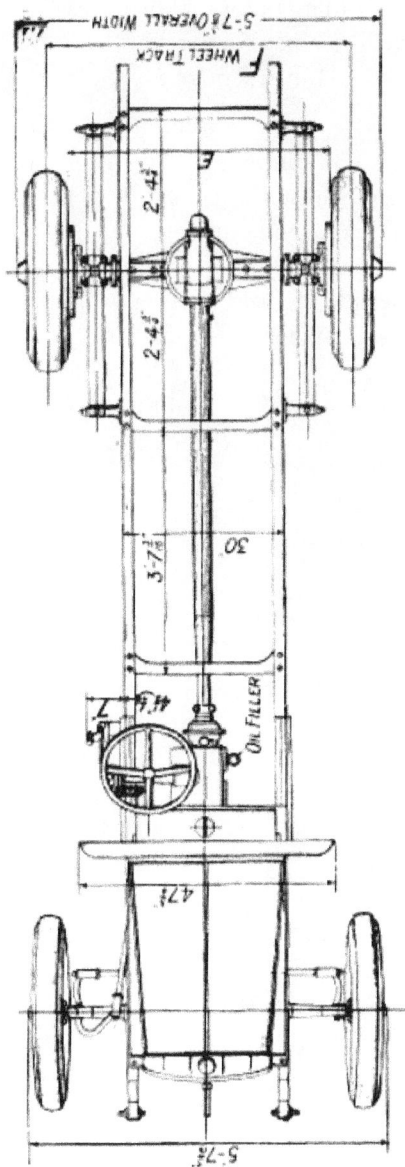

PLAN VIEW OF CHASSIS

Dimensions of A, B, C, D, E and F:—

    Cushion Tyres—110 m/m for 720 m/m front;
                 140 m/m for 720 m/m rear.
  Pneumatic Tyres—33 in. x 5 in. front
               34 in. x 7 in. rear.

	Cushion Tyres.	Pneumatic Tyres
A Height of loaded frame on centre line of front axle (approximate)	2 ft. 4$7/16$ in.	2 ft. 5$5/8$ in.
B Height of loaded frame on centre line of rear axle (approximate)	2 ft. 7$7/16$ in.	2 ft. 4¼ in.
C Top of frame to underside of guard	10$1/16$ in.	10¼ in.
D Top of tyre to underside of guard	3$3/8$ in.	3$3/8$ in.
E Width between wheels	4 ft. 2½ in.	4 ft. 0¼ in.
F Wheel track	4 ft. 8 in.	4 ft. 8 in.

LEONAUR

ALSO FROM LEONAUR

AVAILABLE IN SOFTCOVER OR HARDCOVER WITH DUST JACKET

THE ART OF WAR *by Antoine Henri Jomini*—Strategy & Tactics From the Age of Horse & Musket.

THE ART OF WAR *by Sun Tzu and Pierre G. T. Beauregard*—*The Art of War* by Sun Tzu and *Principles and Maxims of the Art of War* by Pierre G.T. Beauregard.

THE MILITARY RELIGIOUS ORDERS OF THE MIDDLE AGES *by F. C. Woodhouse*—The Knights Templar, Hospitaller and Others.

THE BENGAL NATIVE ARMY *by F. G. Cardew*—An Invaluable Reference Resource.

ARTILLERY THROUGH THE AGES—*by Albert Manucy*—A History of the DEvelopment and Use of Cannons, Mortars, Rockets & Projectiles from Earliest Times to the Nineteenth Century.

THE SWORD OF THE CROWN *by Eric W. Sheppard*—A History of the British Army to 1914.

THE 7TH (QUEEN'S OWN) HUSSARS: Volume 3—1818-1914 *by C. R. B. Barrett*—On Campaign During the Canadian Rebellion, the Indian Mutiny, the Sudan, Matabeleland, Mashonaland and the Boer War Volume 3: 1818-1914.

THE CAMPAIGN OF WATERLOO *by Antoine Henri Jomini*—A Political & Military History from the French perspective.

RIFLE & DRILL *by S. Bertram Browne*—The Enfield Rifle Musket, 1853 and the Drill of the British Soldier of the Mid-Victorian Period *A Companion to the New Rifle Musket* and *A Practical Guide to Squad and Setting-up Dtill.*

NAPOLEON'S MEN AND METHODS *by Alexander L. Kielland*—The Rise and Fall of the Emperor and His Men Who Fought by His Side.

THE WOMAN IN BATTLE *by Loreta Janeta Velazquez*—Soldier, Spy and Secret Service Agent for the Confederancy During the American Civil War.

THE BATTLE OF ORISKANY 1777 *by Ellis H. Roberts*—The Conflict for the Mowhawk Valley During the American War of Independenc.

PERSONAL RECOLLECTIONS OF JOAN OF ARC *by Mark Twain.*

CAESAR'S ARMY *by Harry Pratt Judson*—The Evolution, Composition, Tactics, Equipment & Battles of the Roman Army.

FREDERICK THE GREAT & THE SEVEN YEARS' WAR *by F. W. Longman.*

ALSO FROM LEONAUR

AVAILABLE IN SOFTCOVER OR HARDCOVER WITH DUST JACKET

"AMBULANCE 464" ENCORE DES BLESSÉS by Julien H. Bryan—The experiences of an American Volunteer with the French Army during the First World War

THE GREAT WAR IN THE MIDDLE EAST: 1 by W. T. Massey—The Desert Campaigns & How Jerusalem Was Won---two classic accounts in one volume.

THE GREAT WAR IN THE MIDDLE EAST: 2 by W. T. Massey—Allenby's Final Triumph.

SMITH-DORRIEN by Horace Smith-Dorrien—Isandlwhana to the Great War.

1914 by Sir John French—The Early Campaigns of the Great War by the British Commander.

GRENADIER by E. R. M. Fryer—The Recollections of an Officer of the Grenadier Guards throughout the Great War on the Western Front.

BATTLE, CAPTURE & ESCAPE by George Pearson—The Experiences of a Canadian Light Infantryman During the Great War.

DIGGERS AT WAR by R. Hugh Knyvett & G. P. Cuttriss—"Over There" With the Australians by R. Hugh Knyvett and Over the Top With the Third Australian Division by G. P. Cuttriss. Accounts of Australians During the Great War in the Middle East, at Gallipoli and on the Western Front.

HEAVY FIGHTING BEFORE US by George Brenton Laurie—The Letters of an Officer of the Royal Irish Rifles on the Western Front During the Great War.

THE CAMELIERS by Oliver Hogue—A Classic Account of the Australians of the Imperial Camel Corps During the First World War in the Middle East.

RED DUST by Donald Black—A Classic Account of Australian Light Horsemen in Palestine During the First World War.

THE LEAN, BROWN MEN by Angus Buchanan—Experiences in East Africa During the Great War with the 25th Royal Fusiliers—the Legion of Frontiersmen.

THE NIGERIAN REGIMENT IN EAST AFRICA by W. D. Downes—On Campaign During the Great War 1916-1918.

THE AUXILIA OF THE ROMAN IMPERIAL ARMY by G.L.Cheeseman

THE MILITARY SYSTEM OF THE ROMANS by Albert Harkness